# Bellingham Then and Now

## Kent Holsather
## Wesley Gannaway

A compilation of articles and photographs covering the development of the city of Bellingham from the arrival of the first European settlers to the emergence of a modern city in 1904.

Special sections are dedicated to the T. G. Richards Building, the third courthouse for Whatcom County and the oldest brick structure in Washington State, and the visit of the Great White Fleet to Bellingham in 1908.

2008
Published by the LoneJack Mountain Press, Bellingham, Washington
Printed by Gorham Printing Company, Centralia, Washington

Copyright 2008
With the exception of the photographs from the Center for Pacific Northwest Studies, any part of this book may be copied as long as it is attributed to the authors. For more information contact the LoneJack Press at debnwes@comcast.net

The photographs in this book are the property of the authors except as noted.

ISBN 9780972910149

Library of Congress Control Number: 2008908797

The authors wish to thank the people who contributed to this book.
Bill Becht
Ed Brown
Mac McGillivray
Jim Doidge
Jeff Jewell
George Krienki
Toni Nagle
Ruth Steele
Rosamonde Van Miert
Tim Wahl
Candace Wellman
In Memory of Tripo Costello
Special thanks to Carl and Nicki Akers

Descriptions of property in this book, especially addresses of existing privately owned structures, do not include any right to access. Please respect the privacy and property rights of all citizens.

**About the cover**

These four women are balancing on a log near where the Bloedel swim area is today. Their names and the purpose of their pose have been lost to history but the year is about 1912.
It was at this time that Lake Whatcom was beginning to move from a strictly "working" lake to a place of refuge for the citizens of Bellingham. In their attempt to flee the city's smoky bayside industries for a few hours of leisure, the locals would find the air at the lake to be somewhat more tolerable.
By 1912, White City was going strong as a site for conventions and special events. It had become a popular destination for picnickers as well.
A boating club had been formed and a club house had been built on the lake south of the Larson mill.
Power boat racing was going strong and world speed records were being set.
There were people still living close to the mills on the lake where they worked but with the trolley line extended out to Silver Beach, people began to build homes in the Whatcom watershed even though they were employed down on the bay.
By this time, easy logging around the lake was over and coal mining would eventually cease. As the years have gone by, the mills have disappeared and Lake Whatcom has evolved into a destination for water skiers, fishermen, golfers, swimmers and those who have come to appreciate the watery gem that has provided for our city for so long.

# Bellingham Then and Now

The Richards Brick Building  5

The Great White Fleet  16

Bellingham Then  37

The Boom Years  64

White City  90

Then and Now  106

Maps  187

Bibliography  210

Index  213

**Harvey Haggard arriving in Bellingham at the end of his grueling attempt in the first Mount Baker Marathon on August 11, 1911. The car is going south on Dock Street (now Cornwall Avenue) and has just crossed Magnolia. The construction of the new Federal Building has just started. The downtown Carnegie Library is in the background and the Norwegian Lutheran Church sits on the NE corner of Canoe (now Commercial) and Champion Streets. Jim Doidge collection**

This year, 2008, is the centennial year for many events that occurred in the city of Bellingham, Washington.

1908 was the 50th anniversary of the Richards Building. The Great White Fleet visited the city. The construction of the steam generating power plant on York Street insured adequate power for continued growth of the city.

Significant buildings such as the BB Furniture store and the present-day YMCA building were completed. The Douglas Block was completed.

The city was undergoing a business boom and everyone was feeling prosperous. The Barnum and Bailey Circus and the Buffalo Bill Show entertained thousands. The new Roeder School was completed and dedicated.

In 1908 the Beth Israel Congregation was formed. The new downtown Carnegie library opened. The Sunnyland addition to Bellingham was platted. Diehl and Simpson opened their first automobile store. Whatcom Falls Park was created.

The list is longer, but two events stand out. One helped to shape the future of our city and the other was the "biggest event ever".

The first chapter in our book deals with the 150 year old Richards building and a wonderful attempt to restore it so that it will last another 150 years as a reminder that we all have a history, and that the passing of a person or place doesn't mean that the person or place will be forgotten, especially if there is something that ties us to it, as the old brick building has done for many generations.

# The T. G. Richards Building

The T. G. Richards Building, located at 1305 E Street, just up from Holly Street, is having its 150th birthday this year. The building is in the midst of a major remodel, having been the victim of genteel neglect and remodeling over the last 150 years. For those that wish to keep track of such things, this building is the third oldest visible remnant of our local European history in Whatcom County (the first two are the Pickett house just up the hill and the hole left behind at the Chuckanut Quarry along the shore of Chuckanut Bay).

We owe a great debt to Carl and Nicki Akers for their generosity. We also owe a debt to those local people that have been and are still involved with the current restoration. Without the generosity of the local businesses and members of the Whatcom Historical Society we would most likely have seen this treasure slip into oblivion along with so many of the past relics that graced our city landscape.

Much of our local history took place in this building. Decisions were made in the rooms filled with the civic leaders of the time that are still impacting the city today. Some of these decisions were good and some were bad, but overall, it is probably safe to state that without some of those decisions being made, our city might not exist today. Someone in that building decided to seek out the Kansas Colony to come west and operate the Colony Mill. Someone made the decision to keep the county seat at Whatcom instead of letting Ferndale take it. Someone in that building decided to open the roadways to the interior of the county. Someone in that building made the decision to build the main GN railroad depot in Whatcom instead of letting Fairhaven have it. Plats were signed off so that the city could grow into a central district surrounded by neighborhoods.

1858 was the big year for Whatcom and Sehome. Both villages had a surge in population that overwhelmed the few early settlers. The first plat of Sehome was drawn up in May, shortly followed by the first platting of Whatcom in July. The need for the plats was quite evident as thousands of gold seekers and their camp followers arrived. Gold had been found on the middle and upper reaches of the Fraser River and by the spring of 1858 the word had gotten out in spite of the Canadian authorities attempts to keep it quiet. The result was a steady stream of men arriving by every available boat, sort of an abbreviated California Gold Rush. The newcomers piled up along Bellingham Bay as there was no easy way to proceed north to the gold fields. The business leaders of Whatcom enlisted William deLacy to survey and clear a trail from Whatcom northeast to the bend of the Fraser River north of present-day Sumas. The only other option was to wait for the boat to make a sailing to the Sehome dock and back up to the mouth of the Fraser River and then by sternwheeler up the river to the gravel bars north of present-day Hope, B. C.
Everything had been moving smoothly along until the British owned transportation company that operated the ship decided that the Whatcom businessmen wanted too much money for the charter and decided to go from Fort Victoria instead. Another obstacle was that Governor Douglas of the Hudson Bay Company, stationed in Fort Victoria, was becoming worried that so many U. S. citizens were traveling unimpeded into the interior of British Columbia. Douglas made it mandatory for all newcomers to go to Fort Victoria and register for permission to enter Canada. Many historians consider these actions, along with the fact that deLacy's progress on the trail was taking too much time, to be the reason for all of the gold seekers departure. The truth is most probable that by the end of summer most of the gold had been recovered and the gold rush was busted. The main results were two-fold. The town of Whatcom got a permanent brick building and the Hudson Bay Company lost their charter in Western Canada.
By September of 1858, the populations of the settlements along Bellingham Bay were back down to the number that had been here the winter of 1857. Several of the gold seekers had decided to stay and work in the Sehome Mine or take up claims along the de- Lacy trail. Some of these newcomers would stay around and become the business and civic leaders of the communities, while others would establish communities in the interior of the county.
Governor Douglas had overstepped the authority given to him by the charter granted to the Hudson Bay Company by the government of Great Britain when he demanded that the gold seekers get permission from him to

enter the country. The charter was taken away. However, due to his abilities as an administrator and the organization already in place to deal with any civic structure, Douglas was appointed by Great Britain to be the first governor of British Columbia. This was actually a good thing for the small communities of Whatcom and Sehome as Douglas, despite his dislike of Americans, was actually quite generous in his dealings with the settlers at Bellingham Bay, just as his predecessor John McLaughlin had been with the Americans arriving at Fort Vancouver during the settlement of the Oregon lands a decade earlier.

The impact of the Richards building can only be measured in the early history of the structure. By 1900, the building was in decline along with the neighborhood, and by 1937, when the WPA did the survey of old courthouses in Washington State, the building was much like it is today, another part of the small scale industrial businesses in the area, blending in with the shipping containers and sheet metal buildings, just another old building waiting to be used for storing those mysterious broken and discarded relics of the past. The last few years Carl and Nicki Akers attempted to keep up with the demands of the old building. Carl saved the building from total collapse at one point when the workers pushed in the bottom of the north wall while packing fill along the property line. Carl replaced the basement floor with concrete when it threatened to fall into the cavity between the old pilings.

Prior to the Akers possession, the area immediately around the building was filled with the refuse of the city. Assorted truckloads of garbage including whole cars and some sort of industrial sludge were used to fill in the old shoreline around the building after the city had filled in the area of the old Colony Mill and the little backwater at the mouth of Whatcom Creek. Sanitary Service trucks would back up to the edge of the bluff east of the present post office and dump the day's accumulation of garbage down the slope onto the beach and into the water, continuing a process started in the 1890s. When the city took over the old Bellingham Sash and Door store, it also included the job of stopping the leaching of the oily residue coming from the garbage into the Whatcom Creek waterway.

The Richards building is also an island of history in another way. All of the other old buildings that made up the town of Whatcom have been drastically altered or demolished. The Pickett house is somewhat connected by association and by location but I would consider the Pickett house to be a part of the neighborhood that it sits in. The Richards building is only two blocks away but is a definite part of the "Old Town" of "Mayor" Lou Parberry.
The next oldest building near the Richards building would be the Bellingham Sash and Door building (the RE-Store) but it has been so radically remodeled that it is almost completely replaced. Many nearby private homes date from the 1880s. The Wharf Tavern over the Whatcom Creek waterway is the next oldest, having some exterior changes to a building constructed in 1910.

The land has been reformed, the rest of the original town of Whatcom is gone (except for the now vacant Roth Block), and the mouth of the creek is empty of any mill. Remnants of the dam under the Pickett Bridge are all that remains of the reason for the settlement that now is a major city. The few officers of the county that inhabited the old courthouse have now grown to a small army spread out through a number of large and small offices. The Richards building once served as the county courthouse for an area that included Whatcom, Skagit, Island, and San Juan Counties. Now it only contains a few workers doing their best to keep the building intact for a few more generations.

The building will celebrate its 150 anniversary this year, a "young" time period for the country but still the oldest existing brick building in the Pacific Northwest. As you read of the history of the building you may sense the fact that this was the center of the being of Whatcom. For a period of time perhaps, the people only stayed because the building represented a permanence that couldn't be found elsewhere without some kind of effort. The building only stayed because the effort to remove it was more than the worth, then later it was too late because the town had grown.

Remember this; the town that is here now started to grow around the Richards building because it was and still is, at the heart.  Kent Holsather and Wes Gannaway, September 2008

**The Richards building, c1888. The iron shutters had been installed as protection for all of the gold that was going to be stored in the basement during the gold rush.** Whatcom Museum collection

**The Richards building, 2007. Surrounded by light industry, the back corner was crumbling and the roof leaked. The sewer and drains are plugged. The attic had been used as an artist loft, divided into small cubicles. Jury-rigged stoves heated the interior. The floor was warped due to exposure. Work will soon begin on the restoration. By August of 2008, the brickwork is almost complete and a temporary roof is about to be replaced. The side of the building facing Holly will be completely exposed for the first time in over 50 years when the sewer work commences.**

# THE STORY OF PIONEER WHATCOM'S OLD BRICK HOUSE

The Evening Herald, Fairhaven, Washington, Saturday, March 14, 1903

Excerpts from the article
Making History Today

At 10 o'clock this morning an interesting link in the chain of Whatcom county history was welded by County Commissioners Easton, Slater, and Kline and County Auditor Sybert in the great stone court house in Whatcom. It was the sale of the old brick courthouse building on E street, between Holly street west and 14th street, a building that has often divided honors with the old territorial capitol building in contemporary discussions of the history of our commonwealth.

Many a rugged pioneer has come and gone since this sturdy structure "assumed considerable proportions," and during its upright career not only the history of the Pacific coast, but of the world as well, has received some of its most vital and thrilling pages. It was built at a time when many of the soldiers of the American Rebellion were playing marbles and when some of our greatest generals were hoeing corn or hustling groceries: when Lincoln was a mere up-start in Illinois politics and when Bismarck was a joke in the eyes of Europe.

"The Brick House"

The old two-story structure was never intended for court house or county offices purposes. For that reason the old pioneers never refer to it as the old court house. They knew it in the days when it glowed red with youth as "the brick house," and they know it to this day as the "Old brick house."

From the time in December, 1852, when Captain Henry Roeder and R. V. Peabody heard of the Whatcom creek water power, and came over from Port Townsend in a canoe, until about June 1, 1858, Whatcom was a very simple little burg, whose only connection with the outside world were the sailing vessels that came here from San Francisco to get coal from the Sehome mine, then the only coal mine on the Pacific coast, and canoe carrier mail service maintained by the little-band of "first families." But early in 1858 the reports of fabulous discoveries of the golden fleece on the Fraser river brought mobs that were never counted, but allowed themselves to go down in history as numbering anywhere from 10,000 to 15, 000 ambitious and migratory souls.

This pioneer Bellingham Bay boom, although it was all over by September of the same year, inspired Charles E. Richards and John G. Hyatt to build the first brick structure in the territory, and the inspiration was heeded and materialized before the slump of September set in. The building was built just as it is today by San Francisco contractors who brought the brick, iron, glass and the tin for the roof from San Francisco and finished their work late in the summer of 1858, so that Richards & Hyatt had a large stock of general merchandise on sale therein before the actual holiday season of 1858 showed up.

How long they conducted the store in the building is a matter over which there is a considerable diversity of remembrance among the pioneers of the time, but I have been enabled, with the assistance of Deputy Assessor Charles Donovan, to unearth a transcript of the deed by which the property was conveyed to Whatcom County.

The technical description of the property as recorded in the deed is "lots 12 and 13, in block 5, town of Whatcom," according to the plat of A. M. Poe, made in 1858, but not filed for record until December 25, 1859, and not recorded until June 2, 1883, when it was recorded in the office of County Auditor Charles Donovan, "at the request of Henry Roeder and others, and at the suggestion of the grand jury of Whatcom county."

It is a curious coincidence that the deed by which Charles E. Richards conveyed the old brick house property to the county of Whatcom also lay unrecorded in the county auditor's office for a number of years. This transaction, the sale of the property to the county, was reduced to writing on May 7, 1863, Richards selling the property in consideration of the payment to him of $2,000 in "county of Whatcom script," which was at that time worth about 25 cents on the dollar.

Immediately, soon or late thereafter, the deed was lost or misplaced, and the next mention of it on record is dated June 14, 1871, when it was recorded in due form by the then county auditor, James O. Turner, who added a postscript to the effect that the deed was filed for record May 8, 1863, by County Auditor H. C. Barkhousen, (now of Fidalgo), "and was misplaced until June 14, 1871, when it was found and recorded by me."

The front of the building faces onto E street. At the rear is Center street, which is little more than an alley, but in the early days was a great convience for the court house and for the old Whatcom house adjoining on the north. Like Division street, Center street was but 40 feet wide and extended from 13th street to 15th street. Division, the chief business center of 1882-84, which was retired by the great fire of 1885, was 40 feet wide and extended from 14th to 16th.

In the same year of purchase by the county, 1863, the county offices were established in the brick building occupying the second floor, while the jail was established in the rear of the store room below. Court in the early times was held at Port Townsend, and later at La Conner. In 1884 Skagit county came into existence and the first session of the territorial district court of the third judicial district was convened in the old brick house in that year, Judge Roger S. Greene of Seattle, presiding.

The building was used for territorial and superior court, county office and jail purposes from that time until February, 1891, when the present court house was first occupied by the county officers.

Dignitaries of 1863

The men who held the offices of Whatcom County in 1963 and who accomplished the historic purchase of the Richards & Hyatt brick building for $500 that cost the county $2000 and interest were elected in May 1862. They were: M.H. Offat, commissioner for 3 years; John A. Tennant of Lynden, commissioner for one year--the length of term being decided by drawing straws; James Cavenaugh, Sheriff ; H. C. Barkhousen, auditor; William Moody, one of the members of the Sinclair-Moody Co., which purchased the Bellingham Bay Coal Co (now B. B. I. Co) property from the E. C. Fitzhugh syndicate, county treasurer. The other officers were appointive. Of these Mr. Tawes is still living in Ferndale, Mr. Moody, after the succession of the Cornwall company to the coal miners, went back to California and engaged in the wool business. Mr. .Barkhousen still lives at Fidalgo, near Anacortes, Mr. Tennant who, during his more than two score years' residence, held in succession almost every official position in the county, died at Lynden in 1895 or 1896. I mention these things in connection with John A. Tennant, firstly, because they are interesting facts and everything elsely, because I have been reliably informed by 1863'ers that Tennant really negotiated the deal for the county's purchase of the brick building with which this article has everything to do.

Other County Office Headquarters

Before 1863, when the county purchased the brick house, the county commissioners and other county dignitaries did official work in various places. In the old coal office, in Roeder & Peabody's (Whatcom Milling Co.'s) office, and finally, early in 1857, the first county building was erected on the Roeder trail near the center of block 16, around which cluster other interesting historic facts and possibilities. This original county building was a very modest affair, and was torn down in 1871 or 1872. The county purchased this property, ostensibly for court house purposes, from R. V. Peabody. The deed was dated December 17, 1856; the description of the property is lots 2, 3,6, and 7, block 16, Whatcom, and the price was $4oo. The lots, as the figures indicate form a strip 100 feet wide through the center of the block and extend from F to G street. After 1863 the place became a public cemetery, and it is related that when Nick Dufner dug a cellar for his house on the F street front of the property in 1890 he disturbed at least one tenement of clay that innocently remained in mute witness of the hurry-up methods of Flip-Flap-Flop Watson, who religiously drew his full pay for digging up and removing the silent accompany in the spring of 1889, after which the county sold the property to private parties. The first cemetery was Dead Man's Point, bought from Dan Harris in November, 1862, for $150, by the same commissioners who affected the purchase of the brick house.

First Court in the Brick House

Before the division of Whatcom County and the creation of Skagit County, accomplished in 1883, and consummated by the election January 8, 1884, territorial district court sessions were held in La Conner.

The first session of the territorial district court, third judicial district, therefore, held in the old brick house on E street was convened by Judge Roger S. Greene of Seattle on Tuesday, January 8, 1884, with James F. Cass of Seattle as clerk: James Cavenaugh of Skagit county officiating as sheriff, Stuart Leckie of Whatcom as deputy sheriff, E. C. Pentland bailiff, J. W. Sigfred, now of La Conner, as crier, C. M. Bradshaw, prosecuting attorney of the district, was absent and the court appointed J. I. De Mattos, the first mayor of Whatcom, to conduct prosecuting for the territory and to advise with the grand jury. The first business was the admission of attorneys to practice in the territory and the first name presented was that of I. M. Kalloch, ex-mayor of San Francisco, father of H. K. Kalloch, now residing in Fairhaven. The other attorneys admitted were W. H. Harris, F. P. Sines and W. Stanfield.

The grand jury, eight women and the same number of men was then sworn in as follows: Mesdames M. H. Mayhew, Will D. Jenkins, J. G. Powell, R. F. McPherson, R. Merriam, F. A. Vernon, I. M. Durkee and E. C. Pentland, Messrs., Rufus Sterrns, N. F. Bloomquist, Edward McAlpine, H. Austin, Edward Holtzheimer, S. D. Stuabbs, W. M. Harte and P. A. McMackin. Stearens was appointed foreman by the court and the jury elected Mrs. Powell, clerk. The sessions of the jury were held in Ross & Co.'s City Drug store building on Division Street, destroyed by fire in the following year. The grand jury turned out a grist of indictments a la Seattle but that doesn't belong in this story.

The First Brick Building

The Post Intelligencer recently intimated that the Barns brick building in Olympia was the first to be erected in this territory, but the P.I. doesn't quote dates. I have been endeavoring to settle this controversy once for all and I find that Olympia is out of the question by at least 11 years, Steilacoom being the only rival coming anywhere near disputable dates.

I have just received a letter from Clarence B. Bagley of Seattle, a reliable and as the P.I. admits, a well equipped authority on events of early historical things. Mr. Bagley says: "The honor of having the original brick building rests between the old Bank built in Olympia by George A. Barns in the spring of 1870, an old building in Steilacoom and your own old building in Whatcom. Speaking from memory alone, I should say yours is by far the oldest."

D. E. Tuck, who was at Fort Steilacoom in 1858 and 1859 informs me positively that the old brick building in Whatcom was completed early in 1858 and that according to his recollection, McCaw & Rogers began construction of their one-story brick store building in Steilacoom late in the fall of 1858.

Interest in the Steilacoom building is heightened by the fact that Mr. Rogers, one of the original builders, is still conducting a general merchandise store in the old building.

(Author's note: the brick building at Steilacoom is gone, leaving undisputed the fact that the Richards Building is the oldest surviving brick building in Washington State, and possibly the oldest brick building north of San Francisco.)

## A History of the T.G. Richards & Co. Building

Matthew Aamot

In 1858, the infant settlement of Whatcom experienced a surge in population that has never been seen since. Thousands of miners poured into the town on their way to the Fraser River, and the gold rush that had begun there. A trail was being cut through the woods, and optimistic promoters billed the town as "the next San Francisco". Mercantile interests were quick to take advantage of the miners business, and the partnership of Thomas G. Richards and Company was counted among those entrepreneurs to invest in Whatcom's future. This organization consisted of Thomas G. and Charles E. Richards, brothers; and John G. Hyatt, all of San Francisco, California.

The land on which their "brick warehouse" was built lay on the tide flats at the foot of the hills overlooking Bellingham Bay and the Roeder-Peabody sawmill. Alonzo M. Poe was the original surveyor of the property, which was part of Russell V. Peabody's claim, the partner of Henry Roeder in the sawmill venture established in the early spring of 1853 at the mouth of Whatcom Creek.

**View of the courthouse (T. G. Richards building) at the foot of E street in during reconstruction in 2008. The re-enactors of D Company (Pickett's command) are posted in front of the building during the 150th birthday party for the old courthouse.**

On July 5, 1858 the deed selling "lot number twelve in block five… having a front on E and Centre Street" was recorded, the payment being the sum of $600 to Mr. Peabody. About this time the company bought the middle plot of land between Centre and D streets, where they built a wood framed store building to sell goods from while the brick structure was being constructed. It was here that Hyatt became Whatcom's 2nd postmaster, and "provided a hundred boxes, at private expense, for the accommodation of the public." The post office was later transferred to the brick store, where it remained until January, 1873. Charles continued in this position until January 1, 1860.

It was on July 24, 1858 that the Northern Light publishes the first account of the beginning of the brick building. It is noted that a load of bricks had arrived for the Richards partnership from San Francisco, and that they "are clearing ground for the erection of a two story brick store and banking house." The publisher of the newspaper must have been in a good spot to observe the progress of this task, as it is believed that the Northern Light was headquartered directly across the street from the new store. From a note in Howard Buswell's papers found at the Center for Pacific Northwest Studies, I believe that the person who actually built the store was a man by the name of James Alexander.

In the July 31st edition of the paper we find that the "two story brick building of T.G. Richards & Co., commenced a week ago, is progressing finely. The walls have gone up some six or eight feet, and have received the joist for the first floor. The iron shutters and doors are on the ground, so that no delay will be occasioned in carrying the edifice forward to speedy completion."

On August 28, 1858 the Northern Light had this to say:

"Nearly Finished – The fine two story fire-proof brick building of T.G. Richards & Company on E Street is so far completed as to require only a few finishing touches to render it fit for occupancy, and will be inaugurated by the reception of a stock of groceries and provisions in a few days."

The ad which the company ran that same issue read:
"T.G. Richards & Company
Having completed their new fire-proof
Brick Warehouse, are now prepared to carry on a
Storage and Commission Business.
Cash advances made on consignments and goods stored in our warehouse. "

The bricks used in this structure are reported to have been made in the brickyards of Philadelphia, and shipped as ballast around South America to San Francisco. The entire building is said to have cost the company $8000 in gold to construct. The completion of the store ushered in a new era of architecture for Washington Territory. Without a doubt, the building was constructed before the Steilacoom brick jail or the McCaw & Rogers store in that town. I have researched the Steilacoom "Puget Sound Herald" and found references to the construction of the jail in late 1858, and the store in the spring of 1859. I know of no other claimants to the "first brick building in Washington" title.

The boom in Whatcom went bust almost as soon as it had begun, however. Governor Douglass in Victoria decreed that all miners headed to the Fraser River must stop in Victoria first and pay for a permit. This left Whatcom out of the loop, and the miners quickly faded away. In the words of Editor William Bausman as he left for San Francisco in the fall of 1858, "Whatcom has gone in, and the (Northern) Light has gone out". "Nearly all the best buildings were taken down and carried to Victoria, leaving the two story brick, built by Richards and Hyatt, standing as the solitary monument of departed grandeur." Whereas during the boom lots were expensive and hard to obtain, after the miners faded away it is said the owners had problems even giving them away!

Charles E. Richards and John G. Hyatt continued the business in the building until 1861.

It is a certainty that during the time he was stationed at Fort Bellingham George Pickett had occasion to visit the building, as his home is still located just up the street.

In May of 1863, on the 6th, the county government purchased the brick building for use as a courthouse. Until then, the first and second courthouses were log buildings, and rather shabby ones at that. The move would give Whatcom County the first brick courthouse in all of Washington, and the only one until many years later. Being short on cash, the county issued warrants worth $2000 to Richards as payment for the courthouse. Being short on cash himself, he in turn sold them to one William Moody for between 20 to 40 cents on the dollar. In Sheriff James Kavanaugh's diary from that time, he records August 28th as being the date that "C.E. Richards has sold the remains of everything in his store."

On this day Charles also writes out a power of attorney to Kavanaugh to handle his coal mining claim in Unionville. It appears that he leaves the area, with Kavanaugh and C. Finkbonner left to handle his affairs.

Of John Hyatt's fate, I am not sure. It is known that he took part in the state government starting in May, 1861; perhaps he followed Isaac Stevens to the East and perished in the terrible American Civil War that shook our nation in the 1860s.

The building provided offices for the county treasurer and assessor, and undoubtedly many people important to the history of our county conducted business within its walls. Henry Roeder, Edward Eldridge, and many other founders of our community frequented the building. Roth's "History of Whatcom County" lists many officials who held positions with the county government and who would have occupied offices in the courthouse. During a period of economic recession the courthouse is described as being "now full of goods seized on attachment and on orders of execution." Elections were held with the courthouse as a polling place, and a perusal of the pages of Roth's reveals many heated political campaigns and discussions. The building also sheltered commercial interests, one being a drug store run by Dr. A.W. Thornton. The Bellingham Bay Mail, begun in 1873 by James Powers, was published in a corner of the building. In a later interview Powers recalled that "I would work an occasional prisoner on the press". The jail was located on the bottom floor, and had held such local scalawags such as "Dirty Dan" Harris, imprisoned for killing a man in a brawl. It appears that in 1875 that the building underwent some repairs, and the floors were then partitioned into various offices.

In February of 1877 repairs were made to the lower floor, and in January 1879 the county commissioners decided to build a separate jail to alleviate overcrowding in the brick building. About 1888 the building was pronounced as unsafe for further county business, and business was conducted in the opera house.
A new courthouse was finished in 1890, and stood at G and Ellsworth streets. The brick building was mostly vacant until being sold to the Grand Army of the Republic, a Civil War veteran's organization that also included the Women's Auxiliary.

**The building was photographed during the survey of 1937. This is a frontal view showing the fresh coat of grout that covered the building in order to protect the deterioration of the original material. Much of the material has worn off in the period to 2008. Library of Congress photo**

The James B. Steadman Post #24 occupied this building until 1922, when it was sold to Jasper M. Riddle, a local road and sidewalk construction contractor.

Many sidewalks in Bellingham still bear his name etched into the concrete poured so long ago. Mr. Riddle gave the building to a lodge called the "Junior Order of American Mechanics", of which whose members were not junior in age and had little to do with mechanics. The organization had its lodge meeting room in the upstairs (street level) floor, where Mr. Riddle's grandson Bill Brooks remembers it smelling like "cigar smoke and spittoons". The lower floor was used as a dining room for the occasional meal that followed the meetings.

It was during this time that the Survey of Historic American Buildings came through, circa 1937, and plotted out a complete map of the building. This information will almost certainly be of great service to us in getting it approved for the National Historic Registry.

Later, the Jehovah's Witness church held services in the building through the 1940s.

**A side view of the building taken during the survey of 1937. The lower level was filled in with dirt up to the middle of the lower windows. An excavation in Septemeber of 2008 has uncovered the side of the building. Library of Congress photo**

The more current history of the building, and the key for its eventual preservation, began with Carl and Nicki Akers purchasing the building in 1955 from the church group. Through the years the Akers Taxidermy shop was a familiar icon to Whatcom County sportsmen. After the business outgrew the building, the Akers rented it out to Base Camp, a woodworking shop, and several pottery studios. Carl and Nicki succeeded in getting the building listed with the Washington State Historical Register, and now have offered the building to the Whatcom County Historical Society.

In 2001 the Territorial Courthouse Taskforce was formed to develop recommendations for the eventual preservation of the building. Some sort of interpretive display will be included in the restoration, to chronicle the early history of Whatcom and the various uses the building has seen through the years. The building's history is still being researched and written, with more help needed specifically on the period in use as a courthouse. Anyone with memories or photographs of the building or with more information on its history is encouraged to contact a member of the Taskforce. Partnerships with community groups are being sought to advise and help the project along. It seems that the old red brick building will have a new lease on life, and will be around to witness the next century of Bellingham's history, as it has for the past 144 years.

**County Executive Pete Kremen giving a speech in front of the old courthouse on the 150th anniversary of the building in September of 2008.**

Sincerely,
Matthew L. Aamot

Author's Note :
The history as I have recorded it is based upon research from many sources, including Lottie Roth's "History of Whatcom County", Lelah Jackson Edson's "The Fourth Corner", P.R. Jeffcott's "Nooksack Tales and Trails", Howard Buswell Collection at the Center for Pacific Northwest Studies, and newspaper accounts from "The Northern Light", "Bellingham Bay Mail", and "The Bellingham Herald". Photographs accompanying this article may be attributed to the Whatcom Museum of History and Art, (special thanks to Jeff Jewell) and to the Center for Pacific Northwest Studies, P.R. Jeffcott and Howard Buswell collections. Diagrams and photographs of the 1937 Historic American Buildings Survey may be found on the internet at the Library of Congress website; search for Whatcom County, Washington and the T.G. Richards building. Special thanks also goes to WCHS members Jim and Renee Doidge, Wes Gannaway, and Neill Mullen for their invaluable help in documenting the history of this building. I welcome any corrections and additions to this article, and beg your patience if I may have made an incorrect statement.

## The Great White Fleet was Bellingham's Biggest Event Ever

The history of the U S Navy prior to 1908 was one of a few months of heroic activity among decades of neglect. In the 1780s, during the Revolutionary War, there was no way to compete with the naval forces of Great Britain. Most of the U. S. fleet surrendered to the British. The only significant naval engagement during the war was by the French fleet at Yorktown when they blockaded Cornwallis' army.

After the Revolutionary War, the U. S. realized the need for some sort of coastal protection and built a small fleet of frigates. When the War of 1812 occurred, these frigates harassed the British merchant fleet, capturing over 800 vessels. A few engagements with the British fleet provided some positive PR for our country, but we were still out manned and out gunned. After the war the navy was mainly used for coastal defense and training. The conflict at Tripoli was mainly an action by the U. S. Navy and Marines on land.

During the Civil War, the U. S. Navy played a very important part, doing blockade duty and patrolling the shipping lanes from the Confederate ports to England. The emergence of steel clad sailing vessels and steel hulled monitors made all previous warships obsolete. However, at the end of the war the U. S. still was only concerned with coastal defense. From 1865 to 1885, the Navy was almost completely ignored, along with the other military branches. Even the Army was not modernized. The soldiers fighting the natives in the West were mostly ill-treated and were always short of equipment and food. Much of the time, the soldiers had inferior weapons. Many of the natives at the battle of the Little Big Horn had better rifles than the soldiers. The bulk of the naval forces in the U S consisted of Civil War leftovers, mostly monitors and some sailing vessels. The attitude of the leadership of the Navy was that real fighting vessels had to have sails, and that anyone working below decks such as steam propulsion engineers, were to be treated with contempt.

Around 1885, the attitude of the leadership of the industrialists and many politicians started to change. Talk of going from isolationism to a colonial power started to be printed in newspapers. Manifest Destiny, a term coined in the 1830s to promote westward expansion, soon meant that the U. S. should have some foreign involvement and exploit the natural resources of other countries.

The only way that we could enforce colonialism and protect our ships and property was with a powerful and modern navy. By 1890, with an eye on Cuba and Hawaii, the U. S. was constructing several modern cruisers. The first one, the USS Boston, had spars for rigging sails, but this changed as the older officers retired or died. Soon the Navy had several heavy cruisers and Second Class battleships with 12 inch guns and 20 inch armor that could go 15 knots.

The U. S. now needed some way to gain a few colonies. In 1893, the U. S. took control of the Hawaiian Islands, sending troops to "protect" the property of the sugar cane growers. In 1898, when an incident with the USS Maine occurred in Havana Harbor, the U. S. declared war against Spain. Our navy outperformed the Spanish navy and gained U. S. control over several small countries including the Philippines and Cuba. The U. S. also took possession of several strategic islands in the Caribbean and the South Pacific. The U. S. now had their colonies.

In 1898, the U. S. laid plans to build four modern battleships a year. By 1909, the U. S. had the second largest navy in the world.

By 1900, world politics was quite complex. Expansion using military force was still a way of life for many nations. Many countries were "modernizing" and needed resources not available in their country. Land was becoming an issue. Countries such as Germany and Japan were heavily industrialized and most of the available land was taken up by rapidly expanding cities and more farmland was needed to feed the growing numbers of city dwellers. Competition with other industrial nations was fierce. England was still determined to protect the huge network of colonies and shipping with a large modern navy. Russia was industrializing and most of the other independent nations in Europe, South America, and Asia were also looking to modernize. Exploitation of natural resources was taking place on a bigger scale as larger quantities of iron and other metals were needed. Other materials such as rubber and oil were also in big demand. Countries that had such raw materials became targets of the countries that needed them.

Japan had combined imperialism with military and industrial expansion and soon invaded nearby countries in order to get needed raw materials and cheap labor. In 1904, the Sino-Soviet War showed the superiority of Japan's military, and it was believed by many that the ultimate goal of Japan was complete control of the Western Pacific and all countries nearby.

The U. S. was concerned about these goals of Japan, and President Roosevelt felt that a little waving of the flag from the decks of a mighty fleet of powerful warships would get the attention of any nation. Plans were made to send a flotilla of U. S. warships around the world, and in December of 1907, 16 battleships left Hampton Roads, Virginia, and set sail along the east coasts of North and South America.

A fleet of smaller vessels also sailed south. These torpedo boats (early versions of destroyers) and cruisers were sent to visit ports too small for the larger battleships. In early 1908, word was received at Bellingham that two cruisers would visit the city.

**This Bellingham Herald drawing shows Miss Bellingham greeting the cruisers USS Tennessee and USS California**

On the 9th of April, Bellingham received the cruisers USS Tennessee and USS California. 1600 men and officers were treated to parties and entertainment. Admiral Sebree was greeted by Mayor J. P. DeMattos, Roland Gamwell, Judge Kellogg, A. L. Black, and H. L. Dickerson. Entertainment included visits to White City, skating at Fairyland, and baseball games. Balls were held at the Elk's Club for the officers and at Swanton's for the enlisted men (Swanton's was located on the upper floor of the Fair Market). A reception for the admiral was held at the Cougar Club in the Roehl Block. Lunches for the officers were held at various homes.

Auto tours were given and an informal reception was held for all sailors at the Kulshan Club. The baseball team from the California beat a local team but the men from the Tennessee lost their game. The citizens of the city could visit the two cruisers after paying 25 cents for the short boat ride.

On the 11th of April, the two cruisers left Bellingham and cruised up to Blaine for a surprise visit.

**The USS Tennessee in Blaine Harbor. Allen photo**

**Herald cartoon May 5, 1908**

At this time, it was thought that no battleships would visit Bellingham. However, on the 13th of April, Mayor DeMattos received a letter stating that 8 battleships would visit Bellingham on May 21st. A committee was formed to raise $2500 to pay for the costs of the celebration to honor the fleet.

On April 22, three large flagstaffs were donated from a Maple Falls area mill and arrived in town. A 120' staff was raised at the entrance to Broadway Park, and a similar one was raised at the E. K. Wood mill.

On the 25th of April, the Bellingham Herald had a big spread. *"Thousands will hold carnival when battleships drop anchor. 7288 men aboard-will be the northernmost city in the U S to be visited. A hearty welcome is planned. $5000 to be spent in entertaining the navy. The Fairhaven yacht club is redoing the south side float with strings of lights. Ships to be lit up and in a line and searchlight practice. Holiday to be declared. Ships to stretch 2 miles across bay."*

By the 16th of May, the anticipation was building. Dozens of ads for the coming visit were in the newspapers. All of the organizations were planning some form of entertainment. An advance team of Navy representatives was in town arranging for various activities and supplies. The mayor sent out invitations to all of the other cities in NW Washington and British Columbia to attend the celebration. Several reviewing stands were being constructed along the parade route. Souvenir stands were being set up. Word was received that only 7 ships would visit Bellingham as the USS Louisiana was going to the shipyards at Bremerton early.

**Herald cartoon May 16th, 1908**

**Ad in the Herald May 16**

On the 19th and 20th, tens of thousands of people started to arrive in town. The railroads had put on special trains to carry the visitors, even using flat cars to hold the crowds. A special BB&BC train came from Sumas and Lynden with 11 coaches, 2 flatcars and 2 boxcars full of visitors. The GN agent stated that they had carried over 12,000 people into Bellingham in two days.

**Miss Bellingham greeting the men from the fleet. Herald cartoon, May 20**

As the morning of the 21st dawned, the crowds started to form along the waterfront in order to get the first glimpse of the big ships. By 10 AM, an estimated 100,000 people lined the shore. The Aftermath Club had chartered the SS Chippewa to take 1200 passengers out to the straits in order to view all 16 battleships as they steamed into Puget Sound. Herald ad

**The 16 battleships entering Puget Sound. A. Curtiss photo**

As the ships sailed along, several turned off to visit other cities along the shores. Soon, the seven ships rounded Eliza Island and headed for anchorage along the waterfront of Bellingham. Dozens of smaller craft blew their whistles and the BBIC mill blew their whistle, "Big Ole", as a welcome along with all of the other mill whistles. The noise was said to have been deafening. The Connecticut anchored at 12:45 as the men of the Bellingham National Guard fired a 13 gun volley.

**Sandison photo, Whatcom Museum collection**

**The fleet entering Bellingham Bay. Walker photo, Whatcom Museum collection**

**The fleet at anchor in front of the E K Wood mill, now Boulevard Park. The USS Relief, a hospital ship that cruised with the fleet is surrounded by the smaller boats. Whatcom Museum collection**

Mayor deMattos and the welcoming committee rode the SS Spokane out to the Connecticut and were piped aboard. Other committee members were J. W Loggie, L. H. Bean, Dan McCush, E. P. Y. Day, H. W. Patton, E. B. Deming, G. C. Hyatt, A. L. Black, F. E. Hadley, J. W. Kindall, and H. L. Dickenson. Ensign Atkins, formerly of Bellingham, welcomed the group and escorted them to the admiral.

**The USS Relief, the hospital ship that accompanied the battleships. Sandison photo**

**Admiral Sperry, commander of the Great White Fleet. Naval Archives collection**

Admiral Sperry welcomed the committee and the mayor gave a formal welcome. Chairman Dickenson discussed the details of the entertainment for the fleet visit. Lt. Radley of the Guard discussed the details of the parade to be held the next day. After the welcoming committee boarded the launch, the local ministers went aboard to arrange for services. A banquet for the chaplains was arranged to take place at the Aftermath Club for that evening.

As the ships prepared for visits by the citizenry, thousands of sailors rode special barges to the city docks to begin their visit to the shops and saloons. The Bellingham State and the National Guard bands gave concerts on the jammed streets as the thousands of sailors and visitors swarmed the downtown area. The restaurants were packed and the street vendors busy. The BB&BC arrived with another special train of 5 packed coaches. The GN and NP trains were standing room only. White City was filled with the sailors and their hostesses. The White City pavilion was full of dancers all afternoon.

On the morning of the 22nd, at 10AM, the parade started. Forming at Wharf and Elk (State) Streets, the men marched north along Elk to Ellis and turned back down Elk to Holly, then west to F Street and again reversed direction back to Elk and south to Wharf Street.

*"An estimated 100,000 people lined the parade route. 112 companies of 30 men each paraded from the ships, accompanied by carloads of officers and city leaders. Applause and yelling was thunderous as each unit passed. The morning clouds had burned off and the sun shone bright on the officer's braid and the band instruments. Lt. Radley and his Guard unit came first, then the city police, followed by the admiral in an auto car driven by E. W. Purdy, then the other ship captains and first officers in autos driven by J. J. Donovan and others, then the marines and sailors of the fleet. The 56 piece Marine band from the Connecticut played at the corner of Holly and Elk and then was replaced by the State band when they had finished marching.'*     Bellingham Herald article

**The parade is coming north on Elk Street. Note the battleships in the bay.**
**This photo was taken from the roof of the Bellingham Bay National Bank Building (Pike Block).**
**The McLeod Block and the Pantage's Theater, and the Daylight Block are on the right side of the street.**
**The Alaska Block wasn't built yet, so a reviewing stand was set up on the corner.** Stenton photo

At noon the men had finished the parade route and dispersed for the rest of the day's activities. White City was open to the uniformed men and their ladies. About 2PM, an auto sightseeing tour was given for the officers. At 3PM, the men from the USS Connecticut played the Bellingham baseball team at the fairgrounds. At 8:30PM, Beck's Theater was filled with 1000 men attending the play. At 9PM, the Japanese Society sent up fireworks at Chestnut and Commercial. Many homes in town opened their dining rooms to visitors and the fleet officers. The Cougar Club, Kulshan Club and Elks Club held receptions for the civic leaders, businessmen, and officers of the fleet.

**A view looking up Holly toward the intersection with Elk Street on the morning of the parade. Note the crowds already forming along the parade route. Also note the women on the parapet of the Sunset Block on the left side of the street. The reviewing stand can be seen in the street. Another stand is to the right across from the Exchange Building (with the Atlas Dental Parlor sign on the roof). A third reviewing stand is just out of the photo to the right.**

**A ribbon worn by many of the enthusiastic crowd. Other souvenirs included postcards of the ships of the fleet, scenes of Bellingham and Whatcom County, medallions, various types of hats and scarves, buttons, and pins.**

**The parade left the Sehome dock and marched up Elk to Ellis, turned and came back down Elk and was turning west on Holly Street. The photographer was standing on the NW corner of Elk and Holly. The building on the left is the Exchange Block, just completed in the spring of 1908 (now the YMCA). The Laube Hotel is just down the street. The Admiral is in the auto being driven by E. W. Purdy, president of the First National Bank. The reviewing stand can be seen on the right. Whatcom Museum collection**

Many of the sailors received a special "postcard" made of a 16 inch by 5 inch cedar shingle cut at the Larson mill. Each shingle was banded by a label normally used for a can of salmon processed by the PAF. The "place stamp here" and the phrase "Bellingham Washington, Dear Dad, Here's where they make them" was printed on each shingle by the Parker Printing Company.

The parade is passing the intersection of Elk and Holly. The reviewing stand in Holly Street can be seen on the left. The Marine band from the USS Connecticut is playing as the parade passes. Sandison photo

Detail from the prior photograph. The windows and roofs of the buildings were almost as full of people as the streets were.

**The parade, coming down Holly Street, just approaching Bay Street. Sandison photo**

Another view of the parade marching down Holly toward the turnaround point at F Street. Note the woman sitting on the parapet of the Sunset Block. Stenton photo

**The Parade coming back up Holly from the turnaround at F Street. Sandison photo**

**The marines marching up Holly through the intersection with Canoe Street (now Commercial). The store in the background is the Red Front Store, now the DIGS home furnishings store. Whatcom Museum collection**

**Sailors and their hostesses at the White City fairgrounds at Silver Beach. Stenton photo**

**Dozens of the smaller "Mosquito Fleet" boats took visitors out to the big ships.
Whatcom Museum Collection**

Another photo of the crowds on the deck of a battleship. Whatcom Museum collection

A group of sailors at the McCaddon and Phillips Ice Cream shop in front of the entrance to White City at Silver Beach.

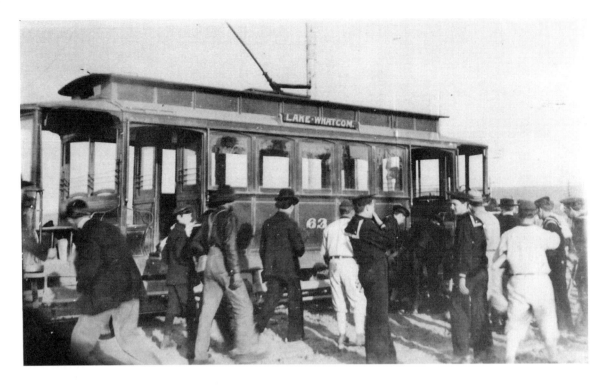

In the afternoon of the 21st, two inebriated sailors were sitting on the front grill of a moving trolley car. They both fell and were run over. Both men died. Their bodies were taken out to the USS Relief.

By midnight it was all over. At 8AM on the 22nd, the USS Connecticut raised anchor and within the hour the fleet was cruising south toward Seattle. Thousands of sailors lined the decks and waved their caps in a salute to Bellingham. By mid-afternoon, workmen were removing the bunting and sweeping up the litter as thousands of visitors streamed out of the city, many to attend the arrival of the fleet in Seattle.

The editor of the Herald said it all: *"To the fleet, bon voyage. Never in its history has the northwest viewed such a spectacle as was seen on the streets of Bellingham yesterday. Not again in a generation, perhaps never again, will such an opportunity come to those whose homes are clustered about this harbor. It marks an epoch in the city's history. Bellingham has been honored, and it has honored itself."*

The USS Connecticut, BB18, was built at the New York Navy Yard in 1904. The Connecticut was designated the Eastern Fleet flagship in 1907 and was the flagship for the Great White Fleet during the trip around the world. The Connecticut was used as a training ship and carried troops during WWI. The Connecticut was scrapped in 1923 in accordance with the Washington Treaty. Whatcom Museum collection

The USS Vermont, BB20, was a Connecticut class ship with 827 men. Built at Quincy, Massachusetts in 1907, the Vermont put a crew ashore at Vera Cruz, Mexico to recapture the U S Customs House in 1911, then carried troops in WWI. The ship was scrapped in 1923.

The USS Kansas, BB21, was a Connecticut class ship. Built at Newport News, Virginia, the Kansas was also at Vera Cruz. The ship was used for training and carrying troops to Europe in WWI. It was also scrapped in 1923. Whatcom Museum collection.

The USS New Jersey, BB16, was a Virginia class ship carrying 916 men. Built in 1906 in Quincy, Massachusetts, the ship was used as a bombing target in 1923.

The USS Rhode Island, BB17, was also a Virginia class ship, and was scrapped in 1923.

The USS Georgia, BB15, was a slightly smaller ship carrying 812 men and only 4 main guns. The Georgia was scrapped in 1923. Whatcom Museum collection.

The USS Virginia, BB13, was built at Newport News in 1906. The Virginia was active in WWI, taking several German vessels as prizes. The ship was used as a target for an 1100 pound bomb in 1923. Whatcom Museum collection. Note the boatloads of visitors on the deck of the Virginia.
An estimated 50,000 people visited the ships in Bellingham Bay on the 21st and 22nd.
All photographs of the ships were taken by the local photographer W. Sandison in Bellingham Bay.


The Washington Treaty was negotiated in 1921 in an attempt to limit the growth of all the navies in the world, particularly the Japanese navy. The treaty specified the number of large warships that could be in a navy, so almost all of the older battleships were scrapped. In 1917, the U. S. had 37 battleships and 33 cruisers. By the end of 1923, the U. S. had 18 battleships and 13 cruisers.


To emphasize the significance of the event of May 1908, a comparison would be if a crowd of 200,000 visitors came to Bellingham to view the Ski to Sea parade. Imagine the affects of such a crowd showing up on a Thursday and going home Sunday. There are approximately 1,000 rooms for rent in the motels and hotels in the Bellingham area. There may be approximately 3,000 seats in the restaurants in the Bellingham area. Would it be overwhelming?

# Bellingham Then

All cities are built the same. They start out as a site with a store or group of dwellings; acquire a post office and some sort of industry, then a steady growth of businesses to support that industry. Eventually the city takes on the business of growth and promotes itself. This self-enlargement becomes a critical component as the city continues to look for ways to increase the tax base. Demand for goods and services create growth, and growth creates a demand for more goods and services.

Bellingham started as a semi-permanent native village and then became the site of a saw mill. There were settlers along the bay prior to the saw mill but they didn't provide the needs required by other settlers, aside from the social aspect. The mill supplied the basic requirements for the establishment of a village, the precursor of the town and city of Whatcom. The mill needed workers, housing, and the essential items such as food, clothing and entertainment. Unfortunately the mill never did well enough to keep a village, and it would seem that inertia kept most of the settlers in the area, whether they were engaged in local activities or just waiting for something better to come along. This was in 1853.

At the same time as the saw mill was being built and operated, a coal mine was opened a relatively short distance away. This mine would be the key factor for the development of a town on Bellingham Bay. The first mine was a failure as far as the making of money was concerned but it brought attention to the possibility of the area, and when another coal seam was located a short distance to the north which proved to be profitable, then this resulted in the establishment of the community of Sehome.

From the beginning, Sehome proved to be the major focus of settlement at Bellingham Bay. Where the sawmill village of Whatcom maybe supported a dozen workers of which only a few could be considered permanent residents, the coal mine at Sehome had around sixty-five workers and would be one of the largest employers in the Territory.

By 1856, Henry Roeder had built the "H C Page" and was hauling sandstone from his quarry in Chuckanut Bay and his sawmill was leased to William Utter. Roeder's partner Russell Peabody was preparing to look for work elsewhere. Utter was cutting boards for the booming town of Fort Victoria whenever he received an order (Roeder had to buy the mill back twice at a Sheriff's sale as no one could make a profit with it).

Meanwhile the coal mine was producing around three hundred thousand dollars annually. At least three ships were hauling coal to San Francisco, around one or two a week. Sehome had a nice dock and a large company store and at least one saloon and several boarding houses and the Sehome Hotel. Sehome got the mail delivery. Sehome would get the telegraph. Sehome would supply the settlers moving inland.

Whatcom's saving fortune was due to the troubles with the natives. The local natives were the Lummi and the Nooksack natives who knew the value of the dollar and would only work for regular wages, while natives from the Northern Vancouver Island area would work for less. These Northern natives were also more aggressive and were feared raiders. For many generations the Northern natives had raided in the Puget Sound area. Eventually there were quite a number of these Northern workers at odd jobs within the Whatcom area and the local natives decided on taking revenge for past actions. These acts, combined with the continuing raids elsewhere on the sound, resulted in the arrival of a command of U. S. soldiers to the sound and the construction of small forts near the settled areas. In 1856, Captain George Pickett arrived on Bellingham Bay with a company of troops and constructed Fort Bellingham west of Whatcom. Pickett was also charged with the clearing of a road to connect the forts around the sound and built a bridge across Whatcom Creek on the flat above the falls at the mouth. The presence of these men resulted in the development of Whatcom as an outpost supply center, reversing the decline of the small village.

By 1858, the two villages had settled down to a relatively normal quiet state, then in the early spring the discovery of gold on the lower reaches of the Fraser River was announced and by early summer there were an estimated ten thousand gold seekers at Whatcom and Sehome.

Visions of vast wealth took shape in the minds of the property owners along the bay and on May 8, 1858, William deLacy platted the town site of Sehome. On July 24, 1858, Alonzo Poe platted the town site of Whatcom for Roeder.

Even though the gold rush fizzled out by the end of summer, many of the gold seekers stayed in the area and went to work in the coal mine or went inland to take up a land claim.

The platting of Whatcom and Sehome was the mapping and establishment of the street layouts. Whatcom had Thirteenth Street, Division Street, and the lettered Streets. Sehome had Front Street and the streets named after company employees of the coal mine. These thoroughfares would be used haphazardly for the next thirty years until the replats during the beginning of the boom years of 1883 through 1892.

After the gold rush of 1858 the two towns returned to some quiet days. Whatcom was still a military town and Sehome went back to mining coal. Most of the buildings constructed of wood during the gold rush were sold off, dismantled, and moved to Friday Harbor or Fort Victoria on barges.

All was quiet in Whatcom until July 26, 1859, when Captain Pickett moved his command over to San Juan Island to deny the British sole occupancy of the island during what is now known as the "Pig War". In 1861, Captain Picket would resign his U S Army commission and join the Confederate forces as his home state was Virginia.

Sehome was the major town on the bay for another decade. However, in December of 1877, the Sehome Coal Mine closed down due to poor mining techniques, and the town had a small exodus of ex-miners, many of them going into the interior of the county to work farms they had acquired while working in the mine.

There is a story told by one of the original settlers, Edward Eldridge, about his walking from Whatcom to Sehome through the woods between the two towns and not seeing one person out and about (this was after the closing of the mine). At one point, the town of Ferndale made an effort to move the county seat as there were more registered voters in Ferndale than Whatcom.

Although the two major industries on Bellingham Bay had closed, there was enough business with the increasing population in the interior of the county that there was a steady population growth for the next decade, the county having a population of about 3100 persons in 1885.

Bellingham started out as a collection of villages that originally weren't going to be villages at all. They simply came into being as needed for the support of two early industries on Bellingham Bay: a saw mill, a coal mine, a few buildings to house the workers and maybe a store for supplies and a place where they could spend money. What more would there be? Many places had these things but could never materialize into towns or villages or grow into large metropolitan areas. So why is Bellingham here?

The first European visitors to Bellingham Bay were the explorers that were looking for a way to get from the Pacific Ocean to the Atlantic Ocean without having to go around Cape Horn or the Cape of Good Hope. The entrance into the Straits of Juan de Fuca was large enough to contain such a passage, so there was some hope for a large navigable passage across the middle of the North American continent. The explorers were also here to collect valuable furs. Otter pelts, and later beaver pelts, commanded great prices in the Far East. A load of these furs could make a fortune for the traders and trappers. One trip from the Northwest to China made a crew enough money to retire for life.

The first visits were by the Spanish in 1791 and 1792. The Spanish drew up charts and named many geological features. Francisco Eliza, commander of the Spanish at their main encampment at Nootka Sound on the west coast of Vancouver Island, was in charge of these expeditions. The second exploration trip to Bellingham Bay by the Spanish was on June 11, 1792. The bay was rough from a brisk wind and caused the two survey ships to run ground. During this time the Spaniards watched as Mt. Baker erupted in the distance.

Any casual contact with another European would be quite rare, but it happened near Bellingham Bay. As the Spaniards were getting their ships out of trouble, the British expedition team under the command of Captain George Vancouver entered the area and met with the Spaniards. The British were here to do some exploring on their own and also to clear up a little problem with the Spanish concerning an attempt to keep the British and other nations out of the area. Earlier, the Spaniards had taken over a British post at Nootka and also confiscated a small ship belonging to the men at the post and took the men to Mexico for internment. Vancouver had been sent to demand the return of the British property and to insure by treaty that all of the west coast was to be open to ships of all nations. The treaty was eventually signed and shortly after the turn of the century the Spanish withdrew to the Californias, leaving the British in sole possession of the region.

The first Europeans to actually stay for any length of time at or near Bellingham Bay were the fur trappers working for the Hudson Bay Company. The HBC had moved its main encampment from Astoria north to the south end of Vancouver Island in the early 1840s when the Oregon Territory was turned over to the Americans. Peter Skene Ogden was in charge of the trappers for the Northwest and his duty was to trap out all valuable animals in order to deprive the Americans any reason to move into the area. A trapping and trading camp was set up on Ten Mile Creek (near the present-day junction of the Hannegan and East Hemmi Roads) and operated there for several years around the mid 1830s (remnants of the camp were still visible in 1858 when the Whatcom-Fraser Trail was surveyed). However, as soon as the trapping was done, the Europeans left.

The original inhabitants of the Bellingham Bay area were the Lummis, Nooksacks and S-mas. Their history went back to the original settlers who had arrived here about fifty-five hundred years ago, according to the ages of the campsites uncovered along the local shores. This was only a few thousand years after the retreat of the last ice age glaciers and it would be assumed that the land wasn't inhabitable before then. These various groups had moved around but always within the boundaries of present-day Whatcom County so that at any time there were probably permanent camps on the shores of Bellingham Bay. While we are going to mention these earlier settlers again in this book, our main story is about the European settlement that has resulted in present-day Bellingham.

After the trappers had gone, the bay was quiet for a few years. As more Europeans moved into the area, mostly to Fort Victoria or Fort Langley, they went farther afield in search of exploitable natural resources. Legend has it that there were fishing camps operating at Point Roberts around 1850. Again, these were not permanent settlers.

Other visitors to the shores of Bellingham Bay were expedition crews. The U S survey team under Charles Wilkes came here in 1841, surveying and renaming most of the geological features. It is well documented that team members came ashore to study the geology and botany of the area.

The Wilkes survey was the result of a political and nationalistic policy known as "Manifest Destiny". This was the idea that the U S was to eventually become the most powerful nation on earth. This policy had been formulated in the 1800s as the country was starting to expand its borders toward the west. Millions of newcomers to our country had created a demand for land. The eastern portion of the U S had been settled and was starting to get a bit crowded, especially in the cities. In the early 1800s, nine out of ten U S citizens were farmers. By the 1840s, this number was dropping, due to several factors. The city workers made more money and could buy nicer items. Much of the land had been over-farmed due to poor agricultural practices, and there had been several recessionary cycles when the banks had failed. Farmers were greatly affected by these cycles as the costs of farming implements rose and the banks called in many of the loans in order to stay open. Many of these farmers were forced to give up their land and seek employment elsewhere, creating a glut of non-skilled laborers competing with recent immigrants from Europe, who were also mostly farmers.

Prior to the 1840s, the U S had developed an expansionist policy that eventually all of North America, including Canada and Mexico, would be one country. The U S had made the Louisiana Purchase and had bought Florida and went to war with Mexico over the southwest. As soon as the Texans had declared independence from Mexico the U S offered to take them on as a new state but the slavery issue delayed that move. By 1940, the push was on to pressure England into giving up the Pacific NW, which was already under joint occupation by treaty.

In 1843, American Settlers formed a provisional government of the Oregon Territory.
In 1845, Oregon created Clark and Lewis Counties north of the Columbia River. These counties encompassed all of the Territory consisting of the land covered by present-day Washington, Idaho, and western Montana.
In 1845, The Tumwater area was settled by U S citizens.
In October of 1846, The Oregon Territory became a U S possession by treaty. The northern border was the 49th parallel.
In 1848, The Oregon Territory became a U S Territory. By 1849, 300 Europeans lived north of the Columbia River.
In 1850, Isaac Ebey settled on Whidbey Island. By this time, over 1,000 settlers lived north of the Columbia River, mostly in the Tumwater, Olympia, and Centralia areas.
In April of 1851, Port Townsend was settled. In November of 1851, Seattle (Alkai Point) was settled.
In January of 1852, Thurston County, which included all of Puget Sound, was formed.

## A CITY IS BORN

The scene was now set for the settlement of Bellingham Bay. Increased activity led to a general knowledge of the area and an awareness of the resources available to the newcomers. Our first European of note to come to the bay was Alonzo M. Poe. Poe was a restless individual who spent much of his life going from place to place looking for that one thing that would make his fortune or at least make him settle down. Alonzo Poe had been one of the major figures in the establishment of the U S in the area of Olympia.

**Alonzo Poe, unknown date. Poe was at Bellingham Bay in September of 1952. He was back in Olympia by 1862, then moved to Napa City, California.**

Howard Buwell papers and photographs #684
Center for Pacific Northwest Studies
Western Washington University
Bellingham, WA 98225

In January of 1852 Poe was appointed U S Marshall at Olympia and was involved in a customs dispute with two ships of the Hudson Bay Company. Poe then was reported as being at Port Townsend in February, leaving that town site and taking passage back to Olympia. By August, Poe was involved with setting up a local government in the Chehalis area. In September Poe was living at Poe's Point in a cabin. Poe's Point was a stop on the upper Puget Sound for the boats traveling from Olympia to Port Townsend and Victoria. The September 9th, 1852 edition of the newspaper "Columbian" advertised Poe as an agent at Poe's Point (Poe's cabin would have been situated somewhere just south of the present-day Amtrak Terminal. Later, when the U S surveyed the area, a white wooden post was placed along the shoreline several hundred feet to the south of Poe's Point. This would become Post Point).

Meanwhile, William Pattle, another ex-California 49er, was working for the Hudson Bay Company in the San Juan Islands cutting spars for the British Navy. Pattle arrived at the bay sometime in October, accompanied by James Morrison and John Thomas. They were surveying the shoreline looking for suitable timber and located a coal seam on the east shore of the bay. Pattle and the others then left to file their Donation claims in Olympia. Now comes the most significant part of the story of settlement on the bay. While on his trip to Olympia, Pattle stopped at Port Townsend. While he was in Port Townsend he stayed at Hastings' store-hotel-restaurant and met with some men that were also staying at Hastings'. These men talked about their search for a waterfall on a shoreline that would allow them to open and operate a saw mill. Pattle told the trio that he knew of such a location, having explored the mouth of such a creek on the northeastern shore of Bellingham Bay. He told them that he would take them to the site for one thousand dollars. At some point Alfred Plummer, the proprietor at Hasting's, took the men aside and told them that they could get the local natives to show them the location for a few dollars, so they told Pattle that they weren't interested in his deal. Pattle then left the area to go file his claim. The men were Henry Roeder, Russell Peabody and John Heath. They had just arrived in the area and were looking for the waterfall on saltwater. Roeder and Peabody had joined forces after meeting in the California gold fields and set up a mercantile, then went on to run a cannery at Sacramento, then left California, traveling to Portland, Oregon. While in that city they heard of a terrible fire in San Francisco and so thought of starting up a saw mill as lumber was in big demand for the rebuilding of the city. While in Portland they met with John Heath who joined the two men on their hunt for the saw mill site. The trio first went to Tumwater to check out that site but a mill was already in operation there so they headed north to look for sites along the shores of the upper Puget Sound (the Tumwater site was already taken by the pioneer Clanrick Crosby, who had purchased the Simmons saw mill at the Tumwater falls in 1850 from Edmund Sylvester. One of Crosby's descendents was Bing Crosby).

**Photographs of Henry Roeder and Russell Peabody, taken some time around the period of their arrival on Bellingham Bay in 1852. Roeder was 28 years old and Peabody was around 45 years old when they arrived at Whatcom Falls. Whatcom Museum collection**

After talking with Pattle and Plummer the men hired some local natives to take them to Bellingham Bay. Prior to the departure from Port Townsend, the travelers were joined by J. D. Hedge. Roeder later related the tale of his arrival in the bay to the historian H. Bancroft in which the men went from Port Townsend in a canoe in two days to the village near the mouth of the creek that Pattle had told them about. They arrived there on the 15th of December, 1852. They were greeted by the local natives and were given permission to construct a saw mill at the mouth of the creek. The natives called the creek Whatcom and this name was also used by the two Europeans. Several documents describe the meeting with the Lummis. Roeder and Peabody met with Chief Chowitzan of the Lummis on the portage at Point Francis and sealed the deal for the saw mill site. The Chief also offered to lend some men to build the mill

Meanwhile, Pattle had gone to Olympia and, in January of 1853, filed his claim along with Morrison and Thomas so that they covered all of the land along the beach that contained the coal seam they wanted to work. Pattle took the northern claim with Morrison the middle and Thomas the southernmost. The coal seam was exposed on the Morrison claim close to the south boundary and almost directly between Poe's Point and what would be Pattle's Point. On a modern map of Bellingham this would be about 100 feet from the water's edge on a line with the middle of the block between Douglas Avenue and Gambier Avenue. Pattle and his partners Morrison and Thomas formed the Puget Sound Coal Mine Association, and in April of 1853, Pattle and company leased the claim to a group of California investors who were represented by William A. Howard. The first ship to haul a cargo of this coal to San Francisco was loaded by wheelbarrow.

When Pattle and company returned to the bay, they discovered that there was activity at the mouth of Whatcom Creek. Roeder and Peabody had started construction of the mill using hired natives to help. After a quick trip to Olympia to look for men and machinery for the mill, Roeder went to San Francisco to get the mill machinery and more men. About a dozen men had already arrived at the mill site, again most likely from Fort Victoria. While in San Francisco Roeder hired millright William Utter before running into Edward Eldridge, an old acquaintance from his days in Ohio, and talked him into coming north. Roeder and Eldridge had been shipmates on the Great Lakes and when Roeder saw Eldridge in San Francisco he renewed the friendship. So when Roeder traveled back north with the machinery, he also brought William Utter, Edward and his bride Teresa and their new baby. Henry C. Brown was a third partner in the mill. Other men that came along to work in the mill were Samuel Brown and Henry Hewitt (Brown and Hewitt were hired in Olympia).

Teresa Eldridge had only been married since February of 1852. She had just given birth to a baby daughter, Isabel. Teresa had come from the last really civilized city on the West Coast, San Francisco (The largest town in Washington Territory was Olympia, with a dozen commercial buildings. San Francisco had a population of around 30,000). She had endured an ocean voyage in the late winter months, and now she had just seen her new home where she would live her days out. It was possibly a wet spring, surely full of insects. The home was a hastily built bachelor cabin sitting like a pile of firewood against the some of the largest trees in the whole world; trees that grew right down to the very edge of a gray colored bay with a cold gray day. She was going to be here with a bunch of rough living men and no other women around. She took one long look around the bay and then went ashore and started her new life as the camp cook and present Queen Mother of this bay area. I am willing to bet that Edward had promised her a fine house, etc., etc.

There is mention of the Dickenson family living on the bay after Roeder and Peabody arrived. Mr. Dickenson worked on the construction of the mill. This family was at Whatcom when the Eldridges arrived in May of 1953. They left soon after, possibly heading north into Canada to get away from the crowds.

At that point in time none of these settlers had made plans to permanently settle at Bellingham Bay, but events would soon happen to change their minds.

Pattle's mine was not doing too well. The coal was of such poor quality that it was only fit for home heating. Possibly only the one shipment was made in 1853 as the first mine lease was given up and another San Francisco company was leasing the property. At the end of the year Pattle abandoned a claim on his property. Most of the coal, around 1500 tons total, came from the Morrison claim.

Meanwhile, the mill was completed in the early summer of 1853 but due to low water in Whatcom Creek there wasn't enough lumber cut to ship to San Francisco. This was the Whatcom Falls Mill, commonly referred to as the Roeder Mill. The Whatcom Falls Mill Company was formed in early 1853 by Henry Roeder, Russell Peabody, and Henry Brown. Henry Brown was a third partner in the mill company but soon left to go back south to San Francisco where he became a building contractor (this is the Henry Brown of Brown's Palace in Denver. This Henry Brown had nothing to do with the coal mine and was only involved with the mill). The first loads of lumber went to build local buildings and some of it went to Fort Victoria (one of the first churches in Victoria and the barracks at Esquimalt were built from some of the lumber cut at the mill).

**A contemporary photograph of the right side of the mouth of Whatcom Creek. The original mill sat about in the upper right corner of the photo. The 1883 Colony Mill sat in the lower right corner of the photo. A foot bridge can be seen on the left side of the photo, about where the original foot bridge was located in 1853. The path went over the bridge and through the mill proper.**

The previous events would have normally meant that most of the settlers would have left the area to look for better prospects. It is very likely that only a couple of families would have stayed to live along the shores. However, in the fall of 1853 two of Roeder's workers, Samuel Brown and Henry Hewitt, were searching along the shoreline east of the mill when they discovered chunks of coal in the roots of a fallen tree. Roeder sent the two men to San Francisco along with 65 tons of coal to attract some investors. By the end of the year the investors formed the Bellingham Bay Coal Company and shipped 400 tons of coal to San Francisco
This finding of more coal had encouraged the settlers to stay on the bay and Roeder, Eldridge, Peabody, J. D. Hedge, C. C. Vail, and W. H. Fauntleroy filed for donation claims, joining Pattle, Morrison and Thomas as landowners.

By the middle of 1854, most of the land around Bellingham Bay was taken up by donation claims. A donation claim was given by the federal government for anyone moving to Oregon Territory. In lieu of payment for the land, a settler could take up a claim and by working the land and establishing a residence on it he would become the owner. The claims along the bay were held by William Pattle, James Morrison, John Thomas, Russell Peabody, Henry Roeder, Edward and Teresa Eldridge, J. D. Hedge, C. C. Vail, W. H. Fauntleroy, Enoch Compton, C. E. Roberts, Henry C. Page, William Utter, John Lysle and wife, Thomas Jones and wife, Maurice O'Conner, and Alonzo Poe. The single men got 160 acres, the families got 320 acres, and Alonzo Poe got 320 acres because he was living in the Oregon Territory prior to 1851.

Pattle's claim boundary took up the land along a line going directly west from the north end of South College Drive, then northeast along to shoreline to a point in line with Abbott Street, then east along a line to the intersection of S. Garden and Garden Terrace streets, then south back to the head of South College Drive.

Morrison's claim was located to the south of Pattle's. His east line ran from the south line of Pattle's claim along the present-day Highland Drive to Douglas Street, then followed Douglas Street in a direct line to the bay.

Thomas' claim was to the south of Morrison's. Thomas' east line followed 14th Street, south to a point between Wilson and Cowgill Avenues, then directly west to the bay.

Vail's claim was located to the north of Pattle's claim. Vail's southeast corner was approximately at the south end of Mason Street and extended north to the intersection of Maple and Garden Streets, then directly west to the bay.

Fauntleroy's claim was to the north of Vail's claim. His east line paralleled Ellis Street north to Fraser Street, then directly west to the bay.

Peabody's claim was along the northwest portion of Fauntleroy's claim. The east line of his claim paralleled Unity Street north to Virginia, then west to a line even with Elm Street.

Roeder's claim was to the west of the Peabody claim. Roeder's north line was parallel to W. North Street with the east boundary along Meridian Street and the west boundary along West Street.

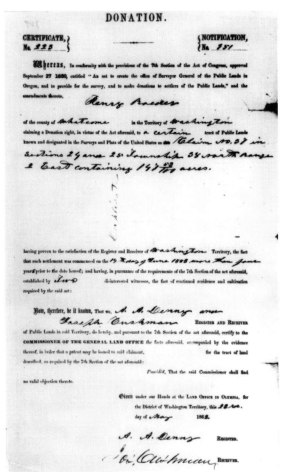

**Henry Roeder's Deed. This deed was furnished when the property owner had satisfied the requirements for taking up a Donation Land Claim.**

Howard Buswell papers and photographs #765
Center for Pacific Northwest Studies
Western Washington University
Bellingham, WA 98225

Eldridge's claim was to the west of Roeder's. Eldridge's northern boundary was along a line with W. Indiana Street, from West Street to a point just a few yards NW of the intersection of Bennett and Marine Drives, then directly south to the bay.

The Compton claim was to the west of Eldridge's with the north line along McAlpine Road going west to the bay.

C. E. Roberts had his claim where the Smith Gardens are today (Mrs. Roberts was driven off her claim when Captain Pickett took the site for the location of Fort Bellingham. Later the claim was returned to her).

Page's claim was directly east of Peabody's with the eastern line being along Iron Street.

The Utter claim was directly east of the Fauntleroy claim with the eastern line at Moore Street.

Jones' claim was directly east of Vail's claim with the eastern line at Racine Street.

The Lysle claim was directly east of the Pattle and Morrison claims with the eastern line at Voltaire Court.

The O'Conner claim was directly east of Thomas' claim with the eastern line along 21st Street.

The Poe claim encompassed most of the land west of 4th Street in Fairhaven south to Willow Road in Edgemoor.

All of the claims are shown on maps in the map appendix.

Shortly after the land rush was over, some of the properties changed ownership. Fauntleroy sold his claim to the new Sehome Coal Mine Company agent, Edmund Fitzhugh, followed shortly by Vail, who also sold his claim to Fitzhugh. This gave total control of the Sehome Coal Mine and the surrounding land to the coal company which would later prove to have a huge impact on the area. When Thomas died in 1854, his estate passed to Daniel Harris. In 1860, the Comptons sold their claim to John Bennett.

Edmund Claire Fitzhugh came north to take over the management of the Bellingham Bay Coal Company in 1854. Fitzhugh was a dashing gentleman from the South and was quite a hit with the ladies. Fitzhugh married the daughter of a Clallam chief by the name of Sehome, and named the coal mine after his father-in-law.

In 1854 Roeder and James Taylor constructed a 42 ton schooner-rigged scow called the "H. C. Page". Roeder, Utter and Taylor skippered the boat, shipping items all over the upper sound. The boat was only the third one on Puget Sound to have a local registry.

In July of 1854, Whatcom County was created from Island County. The county seat was located in Peabody's parlor. Pattle and Roeder both held offices in the new county. The county charter was written and in July the county seat was established on the Peabody claim. This most likely was a major point for some of the settlers staying on their claims. Both Roeder and Eldridge became very involved in the local and regional politics. Eldridge served in the territorial legislature. Two voting precincts were formed. The northern precinct was named Whatcom and the southern precinct was named Ma-Mo-Sea, after Pattle's coal mine. Whatcom County included San Juan County and Skagit County at the time.

Meanwhile, Pattle had been digging like crazy looking for the coal seams but his mine wasn't a big one. Pattle had given another lease to an investment group from San Francisco, in hopes that they could develop the mine into a profitable one. Pattle had really struggled to get this mine to produce, and had dug trenches all over the area looking for more coal seams. His trenches looked like military fortifications, and the area was nicknamed Pattle's Fort by the locals. The mine was worked until late 1858, with about 1500 tons mined in the six years of its life. Pattle never got his fortune in this area, and after helping to get the new county started, headed to San Francisco. After Brown and Hewitt found the big seam at Sehome it wasn't recorded what statement Pattle might have made at the time, but it is probably safe to assume that he had something to say, as he had missed his fortune only by about a half a mile. Pattle knew the importance of this commodity and foresaw the profit and power to be gained from his efforts. How he must have wrung his hands in anguish as he saw his expectations disappear just like all of the other glory holes and mother lodes. William Pattle now joined those other pioneers that stumbled into a situation where they were the instigators of success and wealth in others but had everything sort of slip through their hands (another person in this category was Sutter of California). Pattle seemed to be a sort of never-do-well fortune hunter. He had probably gotten the get rich quick idea from the large amounts of people on the west coast that were in the process of getting rich, but fate had decreed that he merely be the catalyst for the development of the Bellingham Bay area. His remark about a waterfall near his coal outcrops led to the development of the bay and the land around it. His coal outcrop disappeared under apartment and house foundations and his tunnels were buried by sawmill log-yards and railroad tracks as the future generations made their fortunes mining the trees. Pattle's name remains only as the short street up on the hill above the bay, and on the point of land that he dug in (most maps don't even show the name of the point, and only a hand full of people remember the name). Pattle, who was the "father of the bay" so to speak, didn't even get an honorable mention in most of the history books. This honor belonged to those who stayed on the bay and became the founders for today's busy metropolis.

In July of 1859, D. F. Newsom and Seth Doty filed a pre-emption claim on the old Pattle mine and later, about 1861, Doty deeded the mine claims to David Leach, a stockholder in the Unionville mine. This was the last mention of the Pattle Mine. The Unionville mine was the same mine as the Ma-Mo-See. When Richards (the same T. G. Richards that built the brick store in 1858) bought out the mine, he changed the name and established a short-lived town with a post office. In 1861, the town and mine structures burned as the result of a forest fire.

In early 1855, everything was relatively quiet on the bay. The Whatcom sawmill was sometimes operating, the Sehome coal mine was in full production, and the population was slowly increasing. The coal mine was the largest employer on Puget Sound and even Edward Eldridge, who had started working at the mill, ended up going to work in the coal mine because the mill operation was too sporadic. Teresa Eldridge became the manager of the Sehome Hotel (later renamed the Keystone Hotel). In 1855 Teresa was joined by three other settler's wives; Maria Roberts, Mary Lysle, and Elizabeth Roeder, Henry's new bride.
By 1855, the Whatcom sawmill was in debt and had several mortgages on it. The mill had a limited market for its product and even when there was enough water to operate it, there wasn't enough business. Aside from the two dozen buildings in Whatcom and Sehome, everyone else had built a log cabin for shelter. There was some business at Victoria but this wasn't enough to operate the mill full time (the mill never did make a profit. Roeder had to buy the mill back at two different sheriff's auctions, and had to sue lessees at least twice).
In 1854, natives from the tribes on the northern end of Vancouver Island and the Queen Charlotte Islands had raided into the upper Puget Sound, killing a settler on Vancouver Island and then hiding in the San Juan Islands, eventually coming into Chuckanut Bay to the cabin of Joel Clayton and his partner. Clayton escaped but his partner was killed and the cabin burned. The Lummi natives spread word of the attack to the communities on the bay but the Northerners never attacked the settlements. However, two men that were out in a canoe in the bay on watch during the night were killed and their bodies never found. The Northerners then raided throughout the San Juan Islands before fleeing back to their homes.
There was much hatred between the Northern tribes and the local tribes as the Northerners had a history of raiding the Puget Sound area, killing many of the men and stealing the women. In 1855, there were several incidents on the bay with fighting between the Northerners and local tribesmen. At this time the tribes from the eastern part of the territory rose up to drive out the European settlers and even raided and killed several settlers on the lower Puget Sound.
A local militia group was formed with Russell Peabody as the leader and they traveled to the east side to help quell the uprising. A small group of local settlers, led by Edward Eldridge, stayed at Whatcom to guard the settlements and coal mine, which was to keep operating in order to supply fuel for the handful of Navy ships that were stationed in Puget Sound for the duration of the troubles. A blockhouse was built to house the local families at Whatcom. This structure was located at the intersection of what would be Bancroft and Clinton Streets (this area was called Peabody Hill by the locals).
Captain George Pickett and his company of men were stationed at Bellingham Bay in 1956 in order to defend the small community on the bay and to build a road that would connect the military outposts along the eastern

shore of Puget Sound. Pickett decided that the ideal spot for a fort would be on the bluff about five miles west of Whatcom Creek on the Roberts claim. The soldiers drove the Roberts out (the Roberts wouldn't move from their cabin so the soldiers tore the roof off) and built Fort Bellingham, then proceeded to clear a road from the fort through the little settlement at Whatcom Creek and then around the bay to connect with Fort Steilacoom near Olympia. The road was never completed and even the cleared portion on the bay was merely a foot path. There were no horses and wagons at the bay then, thus no need for a wagon road. However, Pickett did construct a bridge over Whatcom Creek above the falls and about 300 feet upstream from the top of the bluff. Eventually a rough road was constructed from the fort around the bay into Sehome. Pickett built a home for himself and his family. He had married a native from the area, as many of the early pioneer men did. Current legends give this young woman the name of Morning Mist, but there are no existing records to validate this. The couple had a baby boy that was named James Tilton Pickett. The mother died soon after the birth and the baby was taken care of by her family.

With the arrival of the soldiers on the bay, the area started to thrive. The soldiers came into the villages to spend their money and the military ordered supplies for the post. Pickett had an office in his home and crews clearing the road and building the bridge. Aside from the footbridge over the mouth of Whatcom Creek at the saw mill, settlers were able to use the path and bridge over the creek at the top of the bluff. Although several settlers, including Roeder and Pattle, had been designated as viewers for roads in the county, there was no money or reason to build anything. Almost all of the settlers lived along the shore of the bay as the only way to get inland was to hire the natives to carry a passenger in a canoe up the Nooksack River (a "viewer" was supposed to survey roads that were to be used for traveling by farmers and settlers living outside of the town boundaries. The viewer would also sign up property owners along the right-of-way to do their share of labor in building the road).

Edmund Fitzhugh was the most important man in the small communities of Sehome and Whatcom. He was a U. S. District Judge and was considered an honorable man although he had a quick temper (he once was tried and acquitted on a murder charge). He had several children by his native wife and being somewhat vain and handsome may have been popular with other women because of his Southern charm. He had many dealings with the other settlers in the area, extending favors and credit to many. Fitzhugh even took a mortgage with Roeder on the "H. C. Page". Fitzhugh was the first sheriff in Whatcom County and in 1857 was the Indian Agent for the bay area.

**Picture of Edmund C. Fitzhugh, taken from a photo album of Territorial judges. Whatcom Museum collection**

A lawyer in California, Fitzhugh came north to manage the Sehome coal mine. Fitzhugh married the daughter of sub-chief Sehome of the Samish Tribe and named the coal mine and town after his father-in-law. Fitzhugh left at the beginning of the Civil War to fight for his home state of Virginia. Fitzhugh married a woman from Iowa after the war but died alone and broke in a San Francisco flophouse in 1883.

The attitude of the natives and settlers was one of friendship and sharing. The Lummis had been in the area for many decades and had several dealings with Europeans in the past. These Lummis also knew the value of their labors and if they didn't just volunteer their services as a gesture of friendship would charge the same as any European for work. Roth related several anecdotes in her book to show the respect that the Europeans and Lummis had for each other. A majority of the European men around the bay took Native wives. Many of these women lived as equals to the European women in the area, becoming integrated socially, although just as many of them were considered "property" and subject to abuses. From the beginnings of the settlement it was illegal to sell liquor to the natives and several European men were arrested by the county sheriff and military officials at the fort. In 1855, after the Point Elliott treaty was signed, the Lummi Reservation was set aside. Many of the Lummis still lived as before, moving around to their established seasonal camps and only living in their traditional homes in the winter. As the reservation boundary included most of these traditional home sites, the Natives had very little adjustment to make. Many of the extended families lived in long houses at the edge of the salt water and on the Portage. Father Boulet visited the area and established a mission there, building a church in 1868 (the oldest surviving church and the third oldest structure still intact in Whatcom County). The Lummis had a traditional camp at the foot of Whatcom Falls, below the bluff where the post office sits today. They continued to visit this site well into the 1900s, using the beach as a campsite when they worked in the hop fields just outside of the city limits (at least until the city started to use the area as a garbage dump). Isabella Eldridge and Lottie Roth were both taken care of by the native women and both were quite fluent in the native language when they were young.

By 1856, the small communities on the bay had settled into a daily routine that involved working at the mill or on small plots of cleared land. The soldiers at the fort worked on their projects or explored the area (some of them would stay in the area when their enlistment was up). Utter, Taylor, and Roeder took turns working the saw mill and hauling cargo on the "H. C. Page". Although several other settlers were also involved with the mill, Utter was usually the head operator and manager. Newcomers to the area included McKinney Tawes and his wife Mary. Tawes worked for the coal mine and they lived in a cabin near Sehome. It was during this time that many of the men in the area were marching around trying to subdue the natives, mostly in the eastern portion of the territory. A list of members of the company is the only one that names almost all of the settlers on the bay in 1856. Forty-four men are on the list, including Russell Peabody as the captain, Charles Vail and Edward Eldridge as lieutenants. When Pickett arrived with his company of 68 men, most of the trouble was over.

**A blockhouse at the Fort Bellingham site around 1895, shortly before it burned. Local banker Frank Handschy is standing next to the structure. The blockhouse burned down in 1897.**

Pickett busied himself and his men with constructing the fort, a palisade 215 feet on a side with two blockhouses on opposite corners. E. D. Warbuss operated the sutlers' store. The buildings, including the headquarters, barracks, and officer's quarters, were built from lumber supplied by the saw mill.
The military road was cleared to the small settlement at the mill site and the bridge over Whatcom Creek was built, being made of long logs laid across the creek with square-cut supports and sawn decking (this bridge was still upright in 1900, when photographs of it were taken by B. Dobbs and Lelah Jackson Edson). Hired by Pickett, Edmund Fitzhugh and other local settlers built the bridge and also did some of the road clearing.
Other bridges were built over Squalicum Creek and a large gulch between F and G Streets (there were a number of these gulches and gullies cutting into the bluffs along the shoreline from Whatcom Creek westward. These gullies were all eventually filled in). The road went eastward along the top of the bluff following the present-day Dupont and Prospect Streets, then went east and south through the village of Sehome. Due to the effort of climbing the bluff to use the Pickett Bridge, most of the settlers walked along the shore, crossing Whatcom Creek on a foot bridge at the mill.

In 1857, there wasn't much in the way of news from the settlements on Bellingham Bay. The Northern natives continued to be a threat and raided other locations on the sound. Several alarms sent the residents at Whatcom and Sehome into the blockhouse on Clinton Street but no one suffered any loss. The big event occurred when Governor Douglas of the Hudson's Bay Company at Victoria learned about the gold on the Fraser and Thompson Rivers and tried to keep it quiet as he knew that there would be a stampede of gold seekers to the area. When a few miners did ship several hundred ounces of gold to San Francisco, the rush was on. Newspaper accounts of the find circulated in California in early 1858 and by April, several thousand men had sailed north. Most of these men landed at Whatcom and proceeded to help construct a trail northeast towards Hope, B. C. on the Fraser River. The trail was to extend north from Hope to the Thompson River, allowing men to cut overland instead of paying for boat passage up the Fraser. At this time, there were between 10,000 and 15,000 men living at Whatcom. Tents and makeshift cabins covered all of the open ground around the community, and a central business district was constructed along the shore and up the bluff on present-day D and E Streets. On May 4, 1858, W. W. deLacy platted the town site of Sehome for Fitzhugh. On July 24, Roeder and Peabody filed their plat of Whatcom, surveyed by Alonzo Poe (see the map index for copies of these plats). Lots in the towns sold quickly, sometimes doubling in price overnight. Many of the arriving men bought up lots for resale at a later time. Construction of a dock for handling cargo was started at the foot of E Street.

When Governor Douglas heard that there were thousands of men trying to get up into the interior of British Columbia, he put forth a proclamation that all miners had to have a permit. Most local historians have said that this was the reason that the miners left Whatcom. It could be that, but at the same time, in late July of 1858, the trail was cut through by deLacy to the Thompson River. However, the trail was very bad in several spots and only passable by foot. Many of the miners attempted the trail and turned back due to the horrible conditions. Also, by the middle of summer the strike was over and many miners were already leaving the gold fields.

One action that had taken place at the start of the gold rush was the rejection of a contract between the settlers and local shipping companies. This contract would have given the shippers a guaranteed access to the docks at Whatcom and Sehome and allowed the shipping companies to carry freight and men from there to the gold fields in exchange for exclusive rights to supply the community with goods and transportation. The traders and community leaders rejected the contract as they felt that they could do better on their own. When the bubble burst, these shippers bypassed the towns on the bay, creating a hardship for many of the business and travelers at Whatcom and Sehome.

In July, there were about 80 businesses at Whatcom and Sehome. A wood-framed courthouse was constructed on Peabody Hill (at E and Clinton Streets). This replaced the makeshift county "office" in the Peabody living room. Most likely due to a lack of professional carpenters and very little funding, this courthouse was quite poorly built, and at one point, the roof blew off in a windstorm and some of the early county documents were lost. Five years later, the county bought the T. G. Richards store and moved the courthouse into the more secure building.

After the gold seekers had all left, the area around the bay was just another backwater without any special consideration. The only constant visitors were the coal company ships that brought in supplies to the company store and left with their cargos of coal. The saw mill was only running part-time and so Roeder and Taylor built the "General Harney", a larger vessel that could ply the Puget Sound waters carrying more cargo. Roeder captained the boat using the occasional native or one of the Hawaiians from the Fort Victoria area as crew members. Most of the time Roeder leased the boat out and looked for other ways to make money. In the early 1860s, Roeder and Warbuss made two trips with a herd of cattle to the upper Fraser River gold fields, using the old Whatcom Trail cleared by deLacy in 1858. Roeder also stayed north for a period of time running a dry goods store in the gold fields.

Henry Roeder was a dandy man, usually wearing his morning coat and polished boots whenever he was walking about town. Somewhat taken with his importance in the community, he frequently was involved in local business deals and politics. Roeder was always ready to greet newcomers to his village and put up many travelers in his home. His best friend in the early days was Edward Eldridge. The two men and their wives were always visiting and were heavily involved with the settlement of Whatcom.

Roeder's other business partner was Russell V. Peabody. Peabody was a bit older than Roeder and Eldridge but seemed satisfied to go along with them in business schemes. By 1868, when Peabody went to California on a business trip, The Roeder-Peabody businesses and the land claims were quite intertwined, so that when Peabody died while in California, all of Roeder's portion of the business dealings and land claims were tied up in probate. Peabody had left a family back east and then started another one when he arrived at Whatcom. These two families would tie up the estate in probate until around 1884, when everything was finally settled.

In the summer of 1859, an international incident occurred. Niegbhoring farmers started feuding on San Juan Island. The Hudson Bay Company claimed that the island was in British Territory and Whatcom County claimed the land for the U. S. The feud escalated until Captain Pickett moved his men from Fort Bellingham to the island, provoking a response from the British. Everything cooled down and the island was jointly occupied until

October of 1872, when the island was declared to be the property of the U. S. Although the troops quit buying supplies for the fort, the local shop keepers were then able to supply the camp on the island.

Although the period of the 1860s was mostly quiet for the people living around the bay, the 1870s were another matter. In August of 1873 the Whatcom mill burned. This would seem to be a large impact on the town of Whatcom, but in fact the mill was a small operation, hiring only a handful of men and probably not even full time. The real affect of the loss of the mill was the fact that it was the only industry in the town, and due to the problems with the Peabody estate, nothing was done to replace the mill.

Meanwhile, the coal mine was having problems with the management and the mine itself. Managers and mine foremen came and left; some good and some bad. The coal in the mine contained a large amount of sulfur, and waste rock in the mine would soak up moisture, creating a condition for auto-combustion of the coal. Several times the mine had a fire in some part, creating unworkable conditions and the mine had to be flooded, then pumped out. These fires meant that the mine was shut down for six months to a year. Concern was shown by the mine owners, and Pierre Cornwall, representative of the owners, made several trips to Bellingham Bay to inspect the mine and determine how best to counter the shutdowns.

The mine opening was originally just along the beach at the projected present-day intersection of Cornwall Avenue and Laurel Street, now under several feet of fill and covered by the street. The second opening took place in 1859 in an attempt to remedy the wet conditions creating fires, and also to intersect the coal vein at a different angle. This opening was located at the projected present-day intersection of Railroad Avenue and Laurel Steet, just south of the old GN roundhouse slab. A third opening was made around 1875 and was at the projected present-day intersection of Railroad Avenue and Myrtle Street. All of these openings were covered by later grading for the railroad tracks that came into the downtown area from the south and went down the bluff to the Sehome and Blue Canyon coal docks.

Eventually, several levels were developed and coal was hauled up inclines to the surface where the coal was stored in a bunker. From there the coal was hauled by a tramway to the dock and loaded into another bunker or directly into the holds of the ships. The coal was mined using the room and pillar method, which left about half the coal in large columns that held the mine ceiling up. The coal was valued at between $12 and $16 dollars a ton delivered to San Francisco. Horses and mules were used to haul the coal carts in and out of the mine, and in later years a steam winch was used.

The mine was quite profitable when it was in operation. During a one year period of operation, the mine produced around $100,000 in profits for the owners. The mine operated for 25 years and produced about 250,000 tons of coal. Nothing is known of the details of the mine operation and costs or profits because all of the records of the company were destroyed in the 1906 San Francisco earthquake.

*He mined coal where city stands*

*Jimmy Guthrie is 80 years old and was one of the first miners who bored under the present city of Bellingham in 1861 going down into the mouth of the tunnel with his lunch box every day where Dock St. and Laurel St. now intersect.*

*"Jimmy" is one of the favored old-timers. He says he "feels just as good as he ever did except not quite so pairt." Although a few months past the eightieth milestone, he walked out to Ferndale and back this last weekend just to visit "Old Abe Green," who used to poke a pick with him into the coal under this city between 1861 and 1873, when they were both on the payroll of the Sehome coal company, removing the first coal discovered on the Pacific coast. "Jimmy" took a trip over to Orcas Island in 1873. He had a little money and figured that he'd take a trip to Australia. Orcas looked so good to him, however, that he's been there ever since. He says that on the original island trip he stuck his pick so far into the island that he couldn't pull it out. So he "just stuck." He now has a small ranch midway between East and West Sound and is hale, hearty and contented.*

*Interesting yarns by the yard relative to the old days, when the population of this location lived solely on a "company street," comprised of two rows of single shacks, can be told by "Jimmy." The coal taken from the mines here was loaded aboard sailing vessels for San Francisco, and "Jimmy" says he can remember that the mariners would come sailing their barks into the dock under full sail instead of trusting to a tug or tow as they do now.*

*"Ay, Mon! but we had some verra gude times I the old days. We'd have a wee-bit uv sports on the green I' fr-root uv the company store. The lads would be a-runnin and jumpin or, perhaps a-throwin horseshoes and we all had a good time" says Jimmy.*

Bellingham Herald, 1909

P.R. Jeffcott papers and photographs #411
Center for Pacific Northwest Studies
Western Washington University
Bellingham, WA 98225

**The Milwaukee roundhouse at the foot of Railroad Avenue in 1910. Locomotives and railroad cars were pushed into the building for repairs or storage. The main Milwaukee line came up the hill on the right side of the structure and went north up the middle of Railroad Avenue to the Milwaukee warehouse on the north side of Magnolia. Torn down around 1974, the building foundation was visible until 2006, when another structure was built at the site. The second Sehome Mine entrance was located just a few feet south of the roundhouse slab.**

**In 2008, these city owned apartments sit over the top of the old coal mine entrance. It is possible that the incline was backfilled near the entrance shortly after the mine was closed.**

In the fall of 1877, Pierre Cornwall came north to inspect the mine, accompanied by an expert engineer on coal mines. The decision was made, and the mine was closed in December. The mine was worked out to the point that the re-occurring fires made the mine unprofitable. Also, due to the opening of the coal mines at Renton, Washington, there was a glut on the market. In January of 1878, the last of the coal was shipped from the bunkers, the machinery was pulled from the mine, and the entrance was closed up. The mine store started advertising a going out of business sale.

Many of the coal miners had taken up donation claims in the county and when the mine closed they went into farming. These farmers would be the main support for the towns of Sehome and Whatcom for several years until another industry could be set up.

**On July 4th of 1873 (Rosamond Van Miert states that it was 1874), a traveling photographer took a photograph of most of the people in the towns of Sehome and Whatcom. They had gathered to celebrate the day of independence and possibly their good fortunes. Years later, many of the people in this crowd were identified by Lottie Roeder Roth. Whatcom Museum collection**

Lottie is number 10. Other prominent locals were Judge George Kellogg and his wife (above numbers 1 and 4), Mrs. and Mr. William Pitchford (5, 6, proprietors of the Sehome Hotel. Mr. Pitchford was also a machinist in the coal mine), Elizabeth Tuck (12, the first white girl born at Bellingham Bay), James Power (19, editor of the BB Mail), John Jenkins (22, proprietor of the Whatcom House), Henry Roeder Jr. (27, killed in an accident), Sam Barrett (30, another early settler at Ferndale), John Slater (31, son of John Slater, early pioneer at Ferndale), and Hugh Eldridge (33, on the horse, son of Edward, born in the hotel when it was named the Keystone).

**Map of the underground workings of the Sehome Mine.**

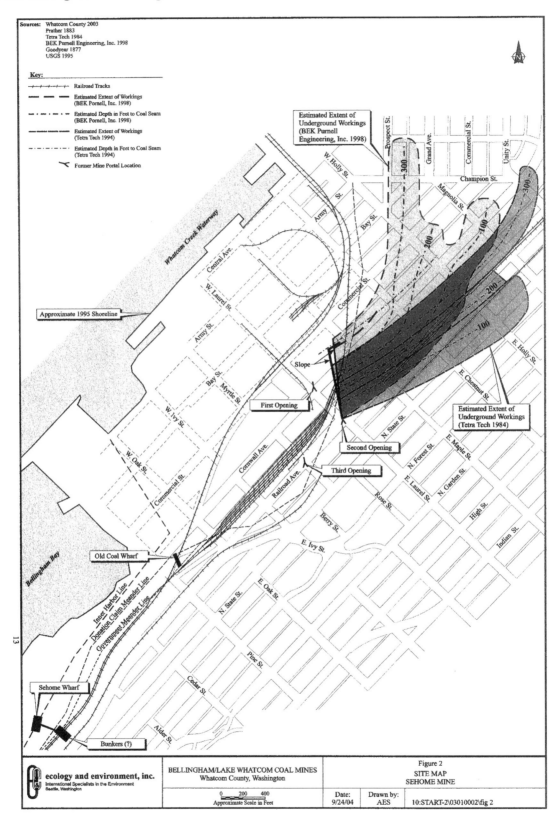

**Map taken from the assessment report for the EPA, September 2004**

**An Early View of Whatcom**

As time goes on, more studies have been done on the physical layout of the shoreline along the settled areas of Bellingham Bay. Also, more information comes to us as more historians do research. It is this way with the site of the town of Whatcom. First platted in 1858, the streets were laid out in the same direction as they are today. An excellent hand-drawn map can be found opposite page 87 of Lelah Jackson Edson's "The Fourth Corner". Our anchor in this drawing is the Richards' building, now known as the third Whatcom County Courthouse and the oldest surviving brick building in Washington. Built in 1858, as described in the special section of this book, the building is quite identifiable in this photograph. The date of this photo is in some doubt, the back is marked in with a date of 1873. Later notations place the date at 1878. Whatever the date, this is the oldest known photo taken on Bellingham Bay. The old Whatcom Mill is not seen in the photo, and we know that the mill burned in August of 1873. However, we also know that a photographer was at the bay in July of 1873 or 1874 as he took pictures at the Fourth of July celebration in Sehome. Another issue is the location of the mill in this photo. The mill site is most likely out of the photo to the right. Whatever the date may be, this is the earliest known photograph of Whatcom. Most of the buildings in the photo were built during the 1858 gold rush. Some were probably completed from the lumber left when the gold rush stopped. Many of the buildings that were constructed in 1858 were moved by barge to Friday Harbor and Fort Victoria. According to the Puget Sound Herald, 31 buildings were moved from Sehome to Fort Victoria. Most of the Friday Harbor buildings burned in a c1905 fire, although there may be some unknown survivors. The buildings in Fort Victoria would have been torn down as the city grew.

In the photo, from left to right, the following structures are visible:

The pilings of the E Street wharf, including a railing that is noticed in the front bottom edge of the newspaper office. This dock was completed in 1858 by workmen waiting for the trail to the Fraser River gold fields to open.

An unknown wood frame building, on pilings.

The Northern Light newspaper office, on pilings. This is the long white building with the one window on the water side. This building was built in 1858, presumably after the arrival of William Bausman, editor and publisher. After the newspaper left in late summer of 1858, the building became the first Whatcom schoolhouse. In the 1860s, the county fair was held in the building.

An unknown white building with a short picket fence on the north side.

Another unpainted building half hidden by the Richard's brick building.

The Richard's building on pilings. See the historical write-up elsewhere in this book.

The Whatcom House hotel on pilings. There was a back entrance to the hotel so that visitors to the courthouse could come and go as needed without going around to the fronts of the buildings. The front of the hotel faced Center Street in 1878.

At this point the little bay at the mouth of the creek starts to curve in towards the bluff. This makes the layout a little distorted as far as measuring the distances between buildings. The view is somewhat off to the side also.

The photographer stood along the shoreline about where Maple Street and Cornwall Street intersect today

The next building is a small building with a reflective roof, probably newer shakes.

Right above this building partly obscured by the brush is the house built by Captain George Pickett when he was stationed at Fort Bellingham. The home was built by Pickett using sawn boards from the Whatcom Mill in 1856.

The next building is another unknown. This building faced present-day D Street. Again, the view is skewed due to the curvature of the shoreline. The building actually sat northeast of a line parallel to the brick building wall. The unknown building just to the east of the last one is a long white sided structure with a light colored roof. Just above and to the right is a shed or outhouse.

The blockhouse for the settlers sat at the middle of the block on D Street between Bancroft and Clinton on the top of the ridge. Nothing can be seen of this structure in this photo.

The next group of buildings, on pilings along the shoreline, are the businesses along Division Street. This street ran up the hill at a right angle to 13th Street (present-day Holly Street), which also later paralleled the facing side of the brick building. Nothing of this street or the buildings is left. Division was on pilings all of the way to the top of the ridge as viewed in other photos in this book. Many of these buildings were destroyed in the fire of 1885.

The house on the top of the ridge above the Division Street buildings is the first home of Edward Eldridge and his family. The first building to the right of the Eldridge home is the original Whatcom Mill office and Whatcom Post Office. The millrace for the mill is just below this building.

Other buildings line the shoreline to the right of the Division Street stores but nothing is known about them during the 1873-1878 period.

## Correction

In our last book, "Whatcom Then and Now", there was a written account of the connection between the Roeders and Samuel Brown, a hired man that worked for the Whatcom Falls sawmill along with Henry Hewitt. These two men, while in the employ of Henry Roeder, were checking out the cutable timber along the east shore of Bellingham Bay sometime in the early part of 1854, and found chunks of coal in the roots of a fallen tree. Soon thereafter, Roeder sent the two men to San Francisco to negotiate the lease or sale of the coal-bearing property. According to various sources but mostly Lottie Roth's history of Whatcom County, the men sold the property and Brown absconded with the money and went to Denver and built Brown's Palace. Again, according to Roth, Elizabeth Roeder visited Brown in Denver at a later date and received a partial payment. Part of this urban legend was that Brown's wife was Molly, the celebrated "Unsinkable Molly Brown" of Titanic fame. In "Whatcom, Then and Now", I debunked the Molly Brown connection.

The Brown of Brown's Palace was Henry C. Brown, a footloose wanderer looking for his fortune. In "Whatcom Then and Now" I stated that Samuel Brown and Henry C. Brown were the same man. This was due to a paragraph in Henry Brown's biography where he mentions being a partner in the Whatcom saw mill with Roeder and Peabody, then selling out and going to California. This sentence, along with the accounts of Lottie Roth, led me to believe the whole story of the absconding of the coal mine proceeds.

I have recently come into possession of more information regarding the sale of the coal mine and subsequent happenings with the proceeds. In the fall of last year (2007) I purchased a copy of the April 1933 issue of the Washington Historical Quarterly, a publication edited by Edmond S. Meany of the University of Washington. Evidently Meany was writing the article "Documents, Foundation of Bellingham" in response to a mistaken identity of Henry Hewitt Jr. as being the son of Henry Hewitt, worker at the Whatcom Falls mill. It seems that Meany gained access to the diary and certain letters of Henry Hewitt and the article is full of references to the coal mine dealings.

Henry L. Hewitt was born in Vermillion, Ohio, and went to the California Gold Fields in 1850 (Henry Hewitt and Henry Roeder traveled together to California). Hewitt then went north to Puget Sound and was involved with the Whatcom Falls mill. Henry and his wife Elizabeth Francis (Smith) had two sons while living in Vermillion. Neither of the sons came west. A grandson, George C. Hewitt, worked for the Asarco smelter in Tacoma after WWI. George Hewitt was the source for the materials used by Meany to write the article. Quotes are from Hewitt's personal notebook.

To paraphrase the main portions of the article, Hewitt traveled from Vermillion in May of 1850 with Roeder and L. Pelton, inventor of the Pelton wheel.

"May 8th, 185[3?] Left San Francisco on board the schooner William Allen bound for Bellingham Bay, W. T. Arrived the 25th of May. I traveled about the Sound trying to convince myself that it was a good country but could not."

"About the middle of August Brown and myself found a coal mine. We got a small cargo out for schooner William Allen. Sold on 9th of December to Calhoun Benham."

"I left for San Francisco on 22d December on board of the bark M. A. Millerll. Arrived there on the fourth of January. I stayed there during the winter settling up for the coal mine. Brown stayed up on the claim. He arrived on 8 and on the 17. I got his money and left for the States on the first of April."

April 1st, 1854. Left San Francisco on board Tarquina for Puget Sound and at Whidbey's Island the 14th of April and on the 19th arrived at Bellingham Bay. I soon got tired of that place."

In May, Hewitt returned to San Francisco on the Lucas with a load of coal and then traveled south through Panama and to New York and then Vermillion in the company of Pelton. Hewitt returned to Bellingham Bay on the 8th of July, 1855. In August Hewitt was one of a party of men including Roeder and Peabody that went to check out the coal mines at Colville, traveling by way of the Nooksack and Frasier Rivers. Hewitt went to Vermillion in December, traveling south via Cowlitz and Portland.

Various drafts, receipts, and billings attest to the financial aspects for the coal mine.

Oct. 1853: A billing by William Utter for $100 to Benham for compensation to Hewitt.
Feb 1, 1854: A receipt signed by Hewitt for $120 from Benham on account to be credited by Samuel Brown.
Feb 28, 1854: A receipt signed by Brown for $120 from Benham on account to be credited by Hewitt.
March 31, 1854: A billing signed by Brown in San Francisco for Alexander McLean to pay Hewitt $740.

In 1859, Samuel Brown brought suit against Roeder, Peabody, and Company to recover money from the sale of the mine. Ironically, Edmund C. Fitzhugh, the mine manager, was also the judge in the case. Brown lost the case and also the appeal.

Various other documents attest to a number of notes signed by Hewitt, Brown, and Benham to the effect that Benham never did pay the total sum of the coal mine transaction to either Brown or Hewitt. One of the last documents is of a bill by Brown against the estate of Hewitt presented to the widow, Elizabeth on August 1, 1862 for $1305. Elizabeth rejected the claim, ending the whole affair.

The possibility does exist that when Mrs. Roeder went to Denver, she went to get money from Henry C. Brown, one of the original partners in the saw mill.

Calhoun Benham was a southern sympathizer during the Civil War and concentrated his efforts toward making California a southern state. The business with the coal mine was most likely a small distraction for him.

The mine eventually was bought by D. O. Mills and his partners. One of the partners in this new group was P. B. Cornwall.

## Then it wasn't so good…

At this time along the bay, perhaps as few as 20 families lived in Whatcom and Sehome. In 1876, Sehome had a population of around 150 and Whatcom had around 120. The 1880 census recorded about 119 persons living around the bay. Times were tough. Most of the men worked at various jobs, either in other parts of the territory or over at Victoria. Another event had taken place in the 1870s that was a hindrance to any development in the bay area. Talk of a railroad coming to the bay had been ongoing for several years but in 1873, war in Europe kept investors away and any thought of a railroad soon died away. This lack of funds also kept the Peabody heirs from investing in any project at the bay. Russell Peabody's estate was held in trust by his brother John, who passed away in 1873, shortly after the mill burned. In 1877, Roeder was able to purchase the mill site outright from the Peabody estate and started to look for someone to build another mill.

Finally, some sense prevailed, and the Peabody heirs and Roeder combined forces to seek out some investors that would come to the bay and build a mill. In 1881, 25 members and their families of the Washington Colony arrived and began to build the Colony mill on the old Whatcom Mill site at the mouth of Whatcom Creek. By late 1882, despite more dissention amongst the Peabody heirs, the mill began to operate.

The Washington Colony was a utopian organization that promoted a socialistic idea of common labor and ownership of property. Each member owned a share of the colony and had equal rights under the charter. This proved to be a problem as major decisions couldn't be made as any one member didn't have enough power to carry a vote. This would prove to be the downfall of the colony, and coupled with several lawsuits brought by the Peabody heirs, the mill operation was never successful. In 1884, the colony broke up and the mill was finally bought by John Stenger. In 1888 the mill was bought by Fairhaven investors as a hedge against the rapid development of Whatcom.

But not all was lost. The development of the mill and the arrival of a large number of settlers to the bay (mostly due to rumors of a railroad) created the need for a modern townsite. A new plat of Whatcom was done in June of 1883 by Henry Roeder and C. J. Pettibone, and soon lots were being cleared and sold. The same year Sehome was also re-platted by E. C. Prather for the BBIC, and the name was changed to New Whatcom. The Whatcom Reveille newspaper started up. In November, the city of Whatcom was incorporated. L. G. Phelps started the Whatcom Bank, first one in the county.

In May of 1885, most of the buildings in the downtown section of Whatcom faced Division Street. Division came downhill from the bluff to the waterline at Holly (13th Street in 1885). Most of the street was built up on pilings as were the buildings. One late evening in May, a fire broke out and before dawn the next morning, much of the business district was a pile of ashes.

Rebuilding started immediately, but not along Division Street. C Street, the next street to the west, would become the new main street of Whatcom.

More talk of a railroad surfaced. The Bellingham Bay Coal Company, now controlled by Pierre Cornwall, held thousands of acres of land that could be quite valuable if a railroad came to the bay. In 1883, Cornwall and his fellow investors decided to start their own railroad and formed the Bellingham Bay and British Columbia Railroad. The plan was to connect the bay with a railroad north to Canada and meet the railroad that was being constructed across Canada. Tracks were laid from the Sehome dock north along the bluff and up the newly platted Railroad Avenue, but the funds dried up and the tracks ended at Chestnut. The first railcar wouldn't be put on the tracks for several more years.

**The main business district of Whatcom along Division Street in 1884. Almost all of the buildings in this picture were destroyed in the 1885 fire. 13th Street ends in front of the Phelps block at the end of Division Street. The Colony Mill dock can be seen running across the back of the buildings. Sehome is in the distance.**

By 1888, as in the past two decades, the arrival of a railroad was a main topic of the bay. The talk soon began to get serious, and by the summer of 1888, the boom started.

# Booming on the Bay

**Lithograph from a promotional booklet produced by real estate investors in 1889. The large building under construction on the right is the Quackenbush Block. This block was one of the first to be built in the central New Whatcom plat. The BB&BC train tracks are going north up Railroad Avenue and the railroad was driving northeast toward Sumas in order to be the first train to reach the Canadian line. A large amount of investor money was being spent. Note the sandstone ridges running north from Holly. Jones and Carlyon had their first real estate office on the SW corner of Holly and Elk Streets. Dozens of newcomers were arriving every day. The city populations would double in three years.**

The newspaper of the day, the Bellingham Bay Express, was printed three times a week. Every edition had several ads promoting land sales, notes about store openings, investors coming into town, of streets being laid and power poles and gas lines going in. Water pipes and sewer lines were laid down even as the stumps were being pulled out of the streets. The building went on day and night, with the windows rattling from the blasts of dynamite used to clear the sandstone ridges and create cellars for the buildings. Several saw mills were set up on the outskirts of town to cut the cedar timbers for planking the streets.

John Stenger's hotel is being built at the foot of Division Street. The photographer stood at the end of 13th Street to take this photo looking west. The Main business center of Whatcom came down C Street and went along 13th (Holly Street).

Looking west on Holly in 2008. The Waterfront Tavern, built in 1910, sits on the left and is the only building still sitting on pilings. Behind the tavern is the old A-1 Equipment Rental building, now the newly opened Chuckanut Brewery. The new public restrooms are on the right, and a private office. The old Bellingham Sash and Door building sits farther west on the right side past the Whatcom Creek outlet. The Sash and Door building was created out of several older original structures dating from the late 1880s.

In this 1890 photo, C Street is on pilings going up to the top of the bluff. The Colony Mill is in the middle. The local natives are camped along the beach below the New Whatcom City Hall. The Colony Dock goes to the left across the mudflats. The rounded roof of the Revielle newspaper building sits along the skyline at the top of C Street. Jim Doidge collection

In 2008, the mouth of Whatcom Creek has been totally altered. Decades of garbage dumping and dredging fill have brought the shoreline out from the bluff for several hundred feet. The building in the center is the back of the Cascade Laundry.

Galen Biery papers and photographs #945
Center for Pacific Northwest Studies
Westner Washington University
Bellingham, WA 98225

The bridge over the Whatcom Creek falls in 1930. The trolley trestle is upstream. The original Picket Bridge was upstream about 100 yards. This modern concrete bridge, built in 1920, replaced a wood structure built before 1895. The Whatcom Chapter of the D. A. R. dedicated the bridge with a bronze plaque. The chapter recently put up a sign recognizing the original dedication. The dam raised the level of Whatcom Creek about six feet. This supplied the water for the Colony Mill via a millrace to a Pelton wheel.

The Picket Bridge in 2008. Note that the dam is gone. Remnants can be seen where it was attached to the bridge. The trail goes along the creek and drops down to the mouth to the old water treatment plant, which is now a salmon rearing pond. The original millrace (a ditch lined with boards in which the water flowed) went out to the edge of the bluff, then dropped down into a pipe to the inlet of the Pelton wheel, making the wheel turn and drive belts to the saw blades.

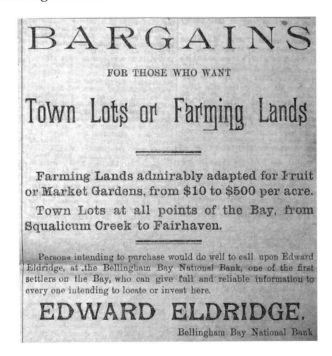
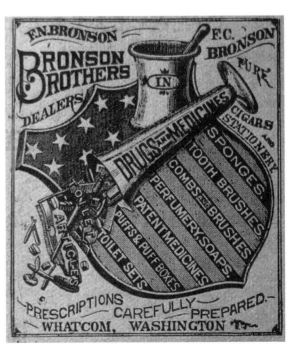

**1891, Bellingham Bay Express ads**

E. A. Hegg took a series of photos on June I, 1891. The three panel set shows the development of the city of New Whatcom. Whatcom and New Whatcom (Sehome) have just merged to form a larger city. This consolidation was done for several reasons: lower operating costs for the city, a larger city could bring in more revenue, a larger city would attract more investment, and finally, the new city was now much larger than Fairhaven. The closest street is High Street, just being laid out. The next Street is Garden Street which is not complete but several houses are along the right of way. The stores face Elk Street. The large building on the left is the new Sehome Hotel. The Orchard Terrace still takes up a large area with its white picket fence. The group of false fronted buildings across the street on the right of the Orchard Terrace are the Morse Hardware stores. One store was just for selling stoves. The Morrison Mill sits out on the mud flats. The GN trestle crosses the bay where it goes back onto the shore near Squalicum Creek on the way north to Ferndale, then Blaine. Whatcom Museum collection

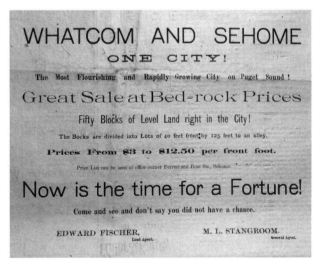

1891 ad for lot sales in New Whatcom. Edward Fisher was a real estate investor and promoter. He built the Fisher Block on Holly. M. L. Stangroom was the manager of the BBIC properties.

**Hegg's second panel of his panoramic view of New Whatcom. The new Sehome School sits to the right facing High Street. The site is now the Laurel Park playground. Down the hill on the left, the back and sides of the Keystone Hotel are white against the dark background. On the right of the photo the rounded roof of the Bellingham Bay Grocery shows. Behind the BB Grocery, the depot for the Bellingham Bay and British Columbia Railroad is being constructed. The large building on the right above the Sehome School is the back of the new J. C. Lighthouse block. Lighthouse was a big eastern investor. The building would house the First National Bank. Along the north side of the bay, the rapidly growing city was also expanding from its origins along 13th and C Streets. The tower of the new Whatcom County Courthouse can barely be seen in the middle distance. Whatcom Museum collection**

**Advertising cards, c1890**

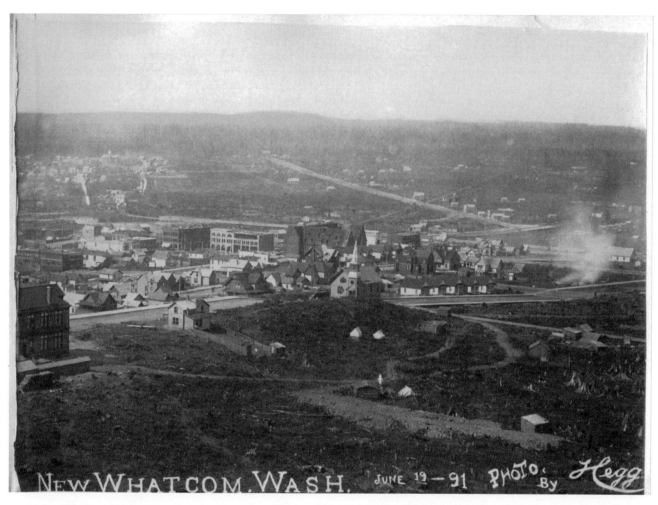

The third panel of Hegg's panorama shows the continuing of High Street towards Lake Street and the York addition. The church in the middle is the newly completed First Presbyterian on the former of Maple and High Streets. Behind the church is the Grand Central Hotel on the corner of Forest and Holly. To the left of the hotel is the Pike Block under construction on the NE corner of Elk and Holly. The building was originally the Bellingham Bay National Bank. Pike bought the building in the mid 1890s at the end of the 1893 depression. Across from the Pike block the newly completed Sunset block stands on the NW corner of Elk and Holly. The new Washington School can be seen in the left distance. The Guide Meridian Street cuts across the upper middle on its way to Lynden. Whatcom Museum collection

By 1888, the Fairhaven Land Company, headed by Nelson Bennett and including C. X. Larrabee, James Wardner, Roland Gamwell, and others, had bought out Dan Harris and then picked up the old Bellingham townsite from Eldridge and Bartlett. Bennett moved in the same business circles as J. J. Hill, the owner of the Great Northern Railroad. Bennett made deals with Hill to get the GN to come north with the idea that Fairhaven would be the terminus. Bennett's first move was to re-plat the townsite and start building a railroad from Fairhaven to the coal fields at Sedro-Woolley. By the end of 1888, the townsite was booming, with workers living in tents until they could build enough homes and boarding houses.

**The Fairhaven and Southern railroad laid tracks in the spring of 1890. The road went up along Chuckanut Creek, then around the east side of Lake Samish, then down toward Sedro-Woolley. The tracks passed through Sedro-Woolley to end at the Cokedale Coal Mine NE of town. Later that year, the Seattle Lakeshore and Eastern met the F&S at Sedro-Woolley and the connection with the GN main line was made.**

The Fairhaven townsite in 1888. The Terminal Building is under construction. The streets are partly laid out and the lots are mostly cleared. Jim Doidge collection

Photo of Harris Street, taken in 1890. The Fairhaven Hotel is being built in the distance. The Terminal building is done, as are several other buildings along the muddy street. Soon the planking will begin. This photo is very popular with the historians, being in nearly every history book written about Bellingham. It must be the mud.

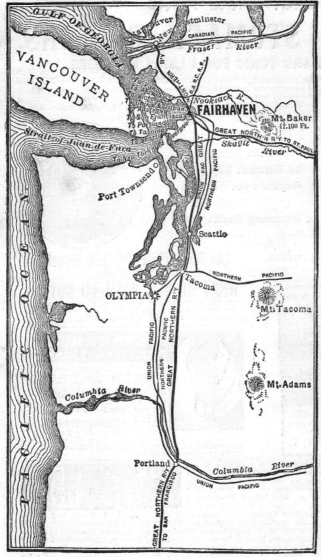

Full page advertisement in the Cosmopolitan Magazine, February 1891

**Dan Harris built his hotel at the foot of Harris Avenue on his Fairhaven plat. The Fairhaven Hotel was renamed the Northern Hotel when Bennett and his partners bought out Harris. The new Fairhaven Hotel would rise up on the hill above and be the finest structure in the city. The Northern would slowly descend into a shabby boarding house for workers at the PAF and finally be torn down. Jim Doidge collection**

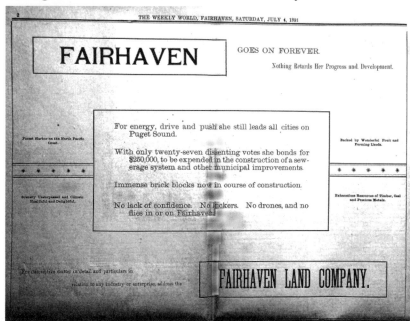

In 1889, the construction of both cities on the bay proceeded at a rapid pace. The closer the railroads came, the more frenzied the activity. The BB&BC was laying rails toward Sumas and hoped to reach the border before the Seattle Lake Shore and Eastern, which was laying track north along present-day highway 9. Meanwhile, the Seattle and Northern was coming north past Sedro-Woolley to reach the southern end of the Fairhaven and Southern. The Canadians were building the Canadian Pacific Railroad and hoped to be at Sumas within the year. The Bellingham Bay and Eastern was working their way around the east side of Lake Whatcom to connect with the Blue Canyon Coal Mine, and later with the SLSE at Wickersham.

The Seattle & Northern, Fairhaven & Southern, and later on the Fairhaven & Northern and the New Westminster & Southern were all under the control of the Great Northern.

The Seattle Lake Shore & Eastern and the Bellingham Bay and Eastern would eventually be controlled by the Northern Pacific.

The BBIC was eventually bought out by the Chicago, Milwaukee, St Paul & Pacific Railroad.

**One of the BB&BC locomotives at the BB&BC depot on Railroad Avenue. The back of the BB Grocery can be seen above the cab. The depot included a hotel. Whatcom Museum photo**

The Bellingham Bay and British Columbia Railroad Company was incorporated on June 21, 1883, and Pierre Cornwall and his partners started work immediately to develop a townsite and lay track north toward a connection with the CPR. A new Sehome dock was built and the old coal dock was abandoned. In April of 1884, the real work began as the grading for the track was started from the dock northward to the top of the bluff. In the last part of 1884, the CPR stated that it had exclusive rights to any railroad in Canada. After laying about 2 miles of track, work on the BB&BC line stopped. In 1888, it was announced that the CPR had no exclusive rights, and the work resumed. The GN, the Milwaukee and the NP also started work northward along the coast to meet with the CPR. Whoever got there first would be in a position of negotiating the best contract. The CPR expressed their intention of connecting with someone at Sumas. The race was on. Two locomotives were delivered to the BBIC in late 1888 and by early 1889, the BBIC had cleared about 12 miles of road. Nelson Bennett was clearing the road for his Fairhaven and Southern from Burlington to Sedro-Woolley and north toward Fairhaven.

On March 1, 1891, the BBIC won the race and reached the border at Sumas. The Seattle Lake Shore & Eastern reached the border a few weeks later. Their depot sat behind the BBIC depot. On May 28, the first CPR train pulled into New Whatcom (with much fanfare and an international incident). Three years later, a passenger could get on the CPR train at the BBIC depot in New Whatcom and get off in Minneapolis.

The BBIC eventually laid over 70 spurs to various towns and logging camps. The main cargo for the railroad was logs and lumber. In October of 1912, the BBIC and all of the equipment was sold to the Milwaukee Line. As the Milwaukee didn't have a line from Bellingham south, rail cars were moved by barges. The barge loading facility operated next to the Sehome dock until the railroad went out of business in the 1970s.

In December of 1890, the Fairhaven and Northern, a subsidiary of GN, pulled into the new depot at Blaine. The New Westminster line was having a great deal of difficulty with grading the railroad across the flats at the mouth of the Nickomekl River and the connection wasn't made for several more weeks.

Eventually, the GN took over the NP and several other railroads. In the late 1970s, GN took over the Burlington and Quincy Railroad and formed BN.

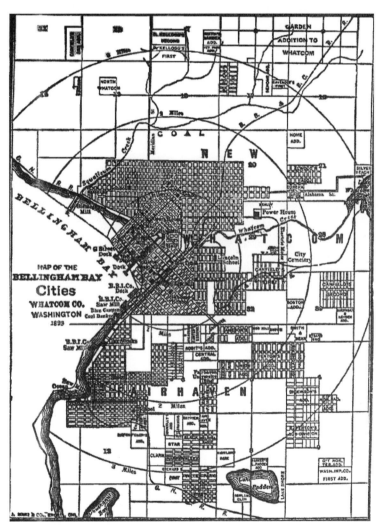

**The Bellingham Bay Reveille had a special edition in December of 1893. This edition was full of information about the wonderful things to be found in the city and surrounding countryside. The paper described the industries and new buildings, cleared farmland, schools, and the rapid growth due to the arrival of the railroads.**

**The local natives camped on the beach below the New Whatcom City Hall. This c1895 photograph shows the trail from the beach up to Dupont Street. The side of the New Whatcom City Hall is at the left edge of the photo. A nice home sits on the bluff where the work center is now. The top of the Fair Market can be seen, now the site of the Mt. Baker Apartments on Champion Street. The Reveille Newspaper building sits on the future site of the intersection of Bay and Dupont Streets. Whatcom Museum collection**

An example of the booming in Whatcom is taken from the May 24, 1890 edition of the Bellingham Bay Express.
"The framework for the addition to the Methodist church is up and the work is going on in a lively manner".
"Mayor Cosgrove's building on Railroad Avenue is being rebuilt as a restaurant".
"The old Bellingham mill has steam up today and is being tested".
"The BBIC is spending over one million dollars on a water works system, railroad machine shops, the saw mill, miles of planking for the streets and sidewalks, and an electric light plant".
"The walls of the new courthouse are above ground level with over 50 men on the construction site".
"Captain Quackenbush has the frame up for his two story building".
"The extension of Holly Street is now cleared and ready for planking".
"The plasterers are now through with their work on the Deeth building".
"The plate glass is being installed in E. B. Belding's new store".
"J. C. Lighthouse is having a brick and stone building constructed at a cost of $35,000 on the corner of Dock and Holly Streets".

Each edition of the Express had several articles on the work in the cities. The paper had ads for hiring all types of laborers and journeymen in all of the construction trades. In 1885 the population of Whatcom County had been 3,098. In 1889, the population was over 6200. In 1890, the population was over 24,000.
On April 18, 1890, the BBIC had the town of Sehome re-incorporated as New Whatcom in order to blend both

New Whatcom and Sehome into one city. In May of 1890, Fairhaven and old Bellingham merged to become the city of Fairhaven. Consolidation was the talk of the day. On December 29, 1890, Whatcom and New Whatcom were consolidated. The talk after that was of the towns of New Whatcom and Fairhaven becoming one city, but there was too much competition between the two cities. It would be another decade before the cities joined together.

**In the summer of 1890 everyone was very busy. The Quackenbush block was finished, the foundation of the Lighthouse Block was started, the DeMattos Block was going up, and Elk Street was being graded along the Boulevard. All of the local newspapers were advertising for skilled and unskilled workers. Dozens of real estate offices were open. Fraternal organizations were forming. Newly formed fire departments were training with new equipment. Contractors from all over Puget Sound were in town to build businesses, homes and streets. Tons of dynamite was being used to clear stumps and create basements and level streets and sidewalks where sandstone ridges had once been. P. R. Jeffcot collection PRJ204, Center for Pacific Northwest Studies**

The same thing was going on in Fairhaven. Hundreds of men responded to thousands of fliers sent out to cities like Chicago and New York looking for new workers and people to buy homes and start up businesses. The Fairhaven Hotel was going up across from the new Mason Block. The Monahan Building was going up just down the block from the newly completed Terminal Building. The Morgan Block and the Waldron Block were being built. James Wardner and J. J. Donovan were having fine homes built.

Charles Roth was in the middle of putting up his Roth Block a few blocks west of the Oakland Block construction site. Roland Gamwell was having his mansion built across town from the site being prepared for the construction of the Bolster home.

The BBIC light company had electricity in 20 businesses by the end of June. Morse's hardware store was one of the first. The gas plant was laying pipe to the newly installed street lamps and dozens of homes. One hundred men were needed to work at the new BBIC Mill. Along with all of this, GN was driving piling and laying rails across the bay. Dozens of ships were bringing in supplies of all types, even food, as the local farmers couldn't produce enough to meet the demand.

By 1890, Whatcom was really booming. The main street of town was still C Street. Hotels, restaurants, saloons, and boarding houses lined the street. New plats were opening up the surrounding area. Smoke from burning stump piles hung in the air as the land was being cleared. Much of the city center was on pilings because it was cheaper and quicker to build over the water than it was to fill in the mudflats. Jenkins' Reveille newspaper office sat at the upper end of the street on Prospect. In a few weeks, the city would merge with New Whatcom to form the largest city on Bellingham Bay. Whatcom Museum collection

**In 2008, nothing is left of the original buildings along C Street. The decking and pilings are long gone. The street dead-ends next to the Maritime Park entrance. Blackberry bushes obscure the view of Prospect Street.**

By 1892, anyone returning to any city on the bay after a two year leave would have been shocked at the changes. The cow paths had been replaced by cleared avenues with sidewalks. Ramshackle wooden structures were now multi-storied brick and stone office buildings surrounded by fancy clothing shops, huge general merchandise, and hardware stores. Families had gas or electric lights, indoor plumbing, factory made furniture, carriage houses, white picket fences, home delivery of food, daily newspapers, and all of the modern conveniences. Men worked in factories where steam power did much of the work and there were electric motors. Wages were such that mothers could stay home with the children while the men worked. The new trolley systems meant that men didn't have to live within walking distance of their place of work. A nickel would take them out to the York addition or along Eldridge Avenue or south along Garden Street. A person could get on the train and go anywhere in the North American continent. Four intercontinental railroads served the cities of New Whatcom and Fairhaven.

Politics, then as now, were all about party affiliations and people talked about the wonders that were to be seen at the Chicago World's Fair. Men working at the saw mills were buying lumber at large discounts and building their own homes on Sehome Hill or along Lake Street or in Happy Valley. Hundreds of families had moved to the area in the past two years. Both New Whatcom and Fairhaven had advertised in the eastern cities.

**A view looking up Holly Street in 1891. A parade is marching down Holly and has halted for the photographer. Jim Doidge collection**

**By 2008, everything has changed. All of the buildings fronting Holly Street are now brick and concrete.**

The first trolley companies were operating in Fairhaven and New Whatcom in 1889. These were small companies and the cost of laying tracks and building cars was too much for these independents. Stone and Webster's Whatcom Railway and Light Company bought out the smaller companies and upgraded and enlarged the system. In February of 1892, the Fairhaven and New Whatcom Railway Company was formed and a small celebration was held. A steam powered generating station on Kentucky Street was built to supply the electricity for the system. Eventually, power plants on York Street and up at Nooksack Falls were built and the company became Puget Sound Power, Traction, and Light.

By 1937, the trolleys had outlived their usefulness. Personal cars and buses allowed people to come and go as they wished, and they didn't have to go to a street with trolley tracks, and after all of those years the trolleys couldn't charge more than a nickel. This photo is of one of the last trolleys to run in downtown Bellingham.

Completed in 1893, the New Whatcom City hall was the showcase of the city. This modern spacious and well appointed building was designed by Alfred Lee and built at a cost of $40,000. After 1904, the building was the Bellingham City Hall until 1939 when the present city hall was completed. Later that year the building became the Whatcom Museum of History and Art. The bell tower burned in 1962 and was rebuilt after a lengthy discussion about saving the building or tearing it down. Luckily, the tower was replaced and the building is now considered one of the finest examples of Victorian architecture in the Pacific Northwest.

By early 1893, the cities of New Whatcom and Fairhaven had grown to encompass most of the land around Bellingham Bay. As seen by the maps, the city limits were out quite a distance. Most of the roads in the downtown area were paved with cedar planking. A dozen banks offered to lend money or save it. Investment firms had many of the offices in the major business buildings. Thousands of men worked in the saw mills and in the woods. Fish canneries were just starting up and thousands of acres of farmland was being cleared.

In June of 1893, the bottom fell out. The price of silver bullion had fallen so low that hundreds of mines in the west closed down. Our dollar was based on the gold standard but the government had been forced by the Sherman Act of 1890 to buy a minimum amount of silver every year and the mint warehouse had tons of silver. When India, which had silver based coinage, declared that it had enough silver and quit buying the bullion, the prices dropped and within a month, many of the banks in Colorado, the biggest producer of silver in the U. S., closed their doors. The panic of 1893 had started. Before long, the panic had spread world-wide, and as the banks closed down, so did the railroads. Within weeks, the stock market had crashed and all investment money had disappeared. By the end of 1893, all growth in New Whatcom and Fairhaven had stopped. Only one bank was still open for business.

From the fall of 1893 until the spring of 1897, not much happened. The Fairhaven Hotel opened to much fanfare but remained mostly empty. The Waldron Block was being built to house the Bank of Fairhaven in 1893 but the bank collapsed and the building wasn't completed until 2006. About the only construction during those years were churches. The Smith Dairy building at 1012 West Holly Street and the Robert Morse home at 1014 Garden Street were also built during the depression. The first construction of Old Main at Western Washington University (also designed by Alfred Lee) was started in 1896 but ran out of funds and wasn't completed until 1899.

By 1897, the banking situation was recovering and business was starting to pick up. Major construction included the Clover Block in 1899 on Holly and Canoe Streets (Commercial). The Clover Block was named after the poem written by the local author Ella Higgenson.

Galen Biery papers and photographs #1461
Center for Pacific Northwest Studies
Western Washington University
Bellingham, WA 98225

In 2008, the Clover Block is home to the Belle Bridal Shop, Azurvedic Health Center, and Sunshine Printing. At one time, the Gage-Dodson Men's Clothing Store occupied the building as shown by the faded name at the back of the building.

**A year later, the Red Front Block was completed across the street from the Clover Block. The Red Front store was a large clothing establishment that competed with J. C. Penney's Golden Rule chain.**

Galen Biery papers and photographs #1104
Center for Pacific Northwest Studies
Western Washington University
Bellingham, WA 98225

**The DIGS home furnishings store now occupies the Red Front store. As seen on the corner of the building above the entry, Commercial Street was originally named Canoe Street.**

As time went on, things got better and better in New Whatcom and Fairhaven. In 1900 there were about 25,000 people living around the bay. Aside from the political bickering between the two cities, everyone was quite happy. In 1901, the state legislature decided to change the name of New Whatcom to Whatcom. The PAF, started two years before, was growing huge and pumping more money into the Fairhaven economy, prompting a slowdown of the city's plunge into a collection of dives and rundown boarding houses. The renewed demand for lumber had revitalized the saw mills around the bay and some days there were a dozen ships loading lumber.

By 1903, prosperity was the key word in Whatcom and Fairhaven. Several canneries were operation in Fairhaven, the mills were all at full capacity (the Loggie Mill would soon break the world's record for the number of shingles produced in a year). The Siemens Mill had opened and was becoming another monster lumber producer. The Morse Hardware Company was the largest such store north of Seattle.

Soon, the talk again turned to consolidation. This was a continuation of the topic first discussed in the boom years of 1889 to 1893. Fairhaven had been the holdout, mostly due to the grand schemes of the Fairhaven Improvement Company under the guidance of Nelson Bennett, but now Bennett was up in the Yukon running the White Pass railroad. His partners had all gone to greener pastures and the few that were left were more concerned with their investments. Everyone realized that there were benefits to one large city instead of two mid-sized ones. Larger cities had more opportunity for commerce and large-scale development. One city was cheaper to maintain and operate than two. A ballot was presented and the votes were cast, and on October 27, 1903, the city of Bellingham was founded.

# White City, the Jewel of Silver Beach

With it's thousands of lights and main buildings of white stucco, the Chicago World's Fair of 1893 became affectionately known as the White City. During a time when most American cities were dimly lit at best, the White City must have radiated like an un-earthly metropolis of the Gods to the visitors who attended the Exposition after dark.

The Fair inspired a generation of entrepreneurial men to fan out across the nation. They would be bringing entertainment and amusement in the form of mini "White Cities" to people who had little time and fewer resources to build for themselves.

By 1900, over 2000 amusement parks operated in the U.S. White Cities were popping up all around the country in such cities as Cleveland, Ohio; Denver, Colorado; Shrewsbury, Massachusetts; Seattle and Bellingham. They were almost always "cookie cutter" in design. The basics usually included a roller coaster, Ferris wheel, a merry-go-round and a dance hall/roller rink. It depended chiefly upon the resources available. Other attractions that were commonly added were slides, penny arcades, fun houses and boat rides.

**Invitation to the grand opening of the Silver Beach Hotel, May 30, 1891.**

*"Grand Summer Resort*
*Mr. Reginald Jones has organized a company and purchased the Silver Beach Hotel and reserve, the wharf, telephone and 500 feet of lake frontage and given a bond of $10,000 to open the hotel in first-class style by May 1, under the management of Mr. Hellener, of Fairhaven. A large band stand and dancing pavilion will be erected, a boat club organized and every arrangement made to make this one of the most attractive and popular resorts on the Sound. Lake Whatcom is noted for its scenery and trout fishing. The hotel is built in first-class style, and its opening will be hailed with delight by the lovers of sport and amusement. An electric railway is one of the improvements contemplated by the company. A number of property holders on the lake have promised land and money to the company on condition they build the road."*
Bellingham Bay Express, New Whatcom, April 7, 1891

The spring of 1906 brought Pittsburgh Plate executive C.H. Chandler to the waters of Lake Whatcom in search of the sizable cutthroat that lurked in its depths. With him was a close friend, William Gwynn, a local realtor. After several hours of fishing, they found themselves drifting in front of the Silver Beach Hotel. Smitten by the property and having an eye for development, Chandler inquired if the land could be bought. Gwynn was able to put the deal together in short order and, as the newly formed "Bellingham Amusement Company", they purchased the property which included the hotel.

The Silver Beach Hotel had worn many hats since it was constructed and had miraculously survived a forest fire that devastated the area including the Silver Beach School but Chandler envisioned it as the center piece of the new development.

William Gwynn was a good realtor but not a rich man so it was Chandler's initial $50,000 seed money that got the Silver Beach White City on its feet.

During the summer months that followed, some of the property behind the hotel was cleared and phase I of the White City was completed. The Silver Beach Hotel, built and opened in 1891, was renamed the White City Hotel.

W. F. GWYNN.
Local real estate man who took Mr. Chandler on Fishing Trip and induced him to invest here.

**Photo of the roller coaster during the visit of the Great White Fleet in 1908. Stenton photo**

A large figure eight roller coaster was built by thrill ride expert Charles Stauffer of Pittsburgh. As construction commenced, he would remark that the fine northwest timber used was of a better quality than anything used in the east and at its completion it was considered one of, if not the best coasters in the State of Washington.

A Ferris wheel over seventy five feet in height was moved from Bellingham to Silver Beach and erected next to the coaster. From its highest point a rider would be able to see several miles down the lake.

The third and final piece of phase I was the merry-go round. It was quite large, housed in a round building, and could accommodate a large number of kids at one time.

The first construction required all of the summer so it wasn't until September 6th 1906 that visitors were allowed on the rides. People were no different in 1906 than they are today when it comes to thrill rides. Over 3000 people rode the roller coaster during the first weekend and the crowds continued to be heavy up until the park closed for the winter.

**Photo of the Ferris wheel during the visit of the Great White Fleet in 1908. Stenton photo**

With Gwynn staying on as the operations manager, Chandler left Bellingham to winter down in Florida but he had a grand vision to add many improvements to the site when he returned in the spring. Among his hopeful additions would be a toboggan slide, house of mirrors, tunnel of love, dance pavilion, rental boats, tennis courts, improved baseball diamond, bear pit and several other mechanical rides.

**1910 view of the entrance to the White City Amusement Park.**

**A lithographic postcard view of the White City grounds. The picture was most likely taken in 1908 when a balloon ride was featured at the park. The three main rides are shown; the Ferris wheel, merry-go-round, and the roller coaster. In this hand tinted card, all of the men with suites on were painted brown.**

The spring of 1907 proved critical for the park as construction flattened out. Chandler's time in Florida probably gave him time to step back from his project and take a more discerning look at its potential. He didn't become wealthy by just dreaming big, he also liked to turn a profit and White City wasn't hauling in huge amounts of cash. He scaled back his ambitious plans and proceeded to go forward in a more deliberate and cautious manner.

White City opened on Memorial Day 1907 with a proclamation by Bellingham mayor Black. He opened the park even though Silver Beach wouldn't be annexed by the city until 1908. A crowd of around 10,000 showed up along with the Washington State Concert Band.

White City was similar to many parks of its day by the way it utilized mass transit. It was a "trolley park". It was built at the terminus of the Silver Beach trolley line. The line was owned by Whatcom County Light and Rail and the creation of the destination hotel and playground prompted them to upgrade their tracks and add additional cars to the run.

Phase II involved the building of a dance pavilion that extended out into the lake on pilings. Its hardwood dance floor was the first of its kind in Whatcom County.

**Considered one of the finest and largest dance halls in the Northwest, the White City Dance Pavillion was a popular destination for the city dwellers. Stenton photo, Bill Becht collection**

Another amenity was the addition of a boat house and rental boats. These boats would prove popular with young couples who would take them out on sunny Sunday afternoons and row them to and fro in front of the hotel.

A "Natatorium" was added near the dance pavilion. A small portion of the lake was partitioned and heated with steam piping. Hot water therapy was somewhat of a rage at that time and was heavily advertised in the Herald and other newspapers of the time.
For the next several years White City advertised special events that would be held on the grounds. "Airship Week" brought Capt. James Moore and his dirigible to the grounds for daring demonstrations. "Fleet Week" brought thousands of sailors from the Great White Fleet to White City and everything including concessions, amusements and trolleys was free to those in uniform but these "events" weren't helping the bottom line.

In 1909 Chandler took over as manager and White city was incorporated. The capital of the corporation was $75,000 and 3000 shares were sold. Chandler saw revenue slipping because of the inability to legally sell liquor. He applied for a license but was turned down by the council. The Women's Christian Temperance Union had some power with the council and it was a year later that Whatcom County went dry.
On May 26th of 1910, the heart and soul of the amusement park was ripped. Mr. Chandler was talking to friends at a nearby store when he faltered and collapsed. He had died from a fatal stroke. His enthusiasm and finances would have to be taken up by others who were probably not as savvy.
White City plodded on and in 1911 the hotel and park were leased to J. N. Noble. With his lease agreement, he promised to keep things running as normally as possible and by the end of the year, the park showed a slight profit of 3 cents a share. That one year probably was an anomaly for the park continued to bleed financially for the rest of its existence.

During the next few years the park continued to offer unique entertainment to its customers. Two bear cubs were brought to the park and placed in the bear pit. They were quite an attraction while they were young and cute but the novelty wore off as they matured and had become more difficult to handle. Their fate was sealed and a Herald article read as follows: Two black bears held captive at White City were killed and are hanging in front of Frye & Company's market downtown. The fur and meat were being sold for "fancy" prices.
Longfellow's play, "Hiawatha" was performed on a barge anchored off the shore of the hotel and hundreds of people attended the performance. The barge was also used on 4th of July nights as a fire works platform.
One of the more tragic events that happened at the park involved a trained dog that jumped from a balloon gondola with a parachute on. The parachute opened just fine but the dog landed in the lake and the chute landed on top of him. He drowned in front of many parents and children before rescuers could get to him. There were a lot of distraught children that day.

Noble ran the hotel and White City during the summer of 1911, but by October he opted out of the five year lease. The White City continued under seasonal agreements for seven more years. During this time the Silver Beach Hotel resorted back to its original name.

Crowds were quite large during the early years of the park but most of the larger days were generated by company picnics, G.A.R. encampments and Chautauqua retreats but even these dried up towards the end. The increasing dominance of the automobile made it possible for families to choose other destinations of interest. This new freedom of the road combined with the limited attractions at the park helped spell its doom.

**Herald Ad, 1912**

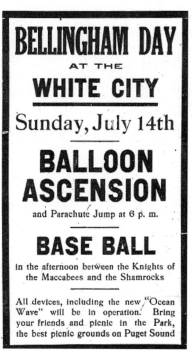

During World War 1 the park was seldom visited except for the occasional company picnic and family outings. As the financing dwindled, the park fell into disrepair and in January 1922 the property was purchased by the Pacific Atomized Fuel Company. A coal shaft was started and the hotel was used as a bunk house for the miners. During this time the roller coaster was torn down and its wood sold to local residents for building garages, chicken coops and such. The bigger timbers were thought to have been used for mine shoring.
The merry-go-round was sold and taken to Ketchikan, Alaska for a time and later sold to an amusement park in Prince George, B.C.
The fate of the Ferris wheel and the other park buildings is murky at best but the round building that held the merry-go-round was used as a blacksmith shop for the mining company.
The mining venture never really panned out and the site was abandoned. Having cut the building in half and stripping all the luxuries from the rooms, they left the once stately hotel in a decidedly derelict condition.
In 1930, Ethel Henika ordered the hotel to be torn down. She had acquired the building as a partial payment for the debts that the park had built up over the years.
Some people in the county have claimed that the wood from the building was used in the construction of their homes but nobody really knows where most of the material went.
The coal mine shaft was finally sealed in the 50s because it posed a danger to kids in the area.
The site is now a completely residential area with single family houses and condos along the shore but I've heard if you walk by the site on a warm August night and listen very carefully, you just might hear the laughter of people and the faint rumble of a coaster as it banks for home.

A view taken from the top of the White City roller coaster looking southwest across the business district of Silver Beach. The Larsen Mill can be seen across the lake. The Silver Beach store now occupies the vacant corner lot. Whatcom Museum collection

1911 ad for the balloon ride at White City. During one of these rides a dog wearing a parachute was dropped and safely landed but drowned in the lake.

Many of the trolleys in Bellingham carried signs displaying special events at White City. The trolley cars made a lot of money hauling people up the hill to the amusement park.

**1911 advertisement for a Memorial Day celebration at White City.**

A major factor in the demise of the White City Park was that so much of the food items, trinkets, rides and admissions were free.

*"Food Supply at the White City is Exhausted
Although the citizens in charge of the reception of the sailors at the White City prepared food for thousands of people during the three days devoted to that purpose, they found at an early hour last evening that the larders were bare. The gigantic task of again replenishing the stocks caused extra labor for all the sub-committees and all the people that could be pressed into the service during the night. By the time the gates were again thrown open to the crowds at 10 o'clock this morning, a large quantity of things good for the inner man were ready for serving. Long before the parade of the day was in line the jackies on shore leave boarded the cars for the lake resort, and when the gates were opened trooped in to enjoy the free provisions for their entertainment. The resort has been one of the busiest places in the city ever since the arrival of the Atlantic fleet yesterday, and will continue to be in the lead of amusement centers until the close of the sailor's dance in the pavilion at 12 o'clock tonight."* Bellingham Herald, May 22, 1908

**(MEMORIAL DAY)**

## Fine Program of Entertainment

All Surviving Veterans and Their Families Will Be Welcomed Free of Charge

PROGRAM AS FOLLOWS:
All amusement devices will be in operation. Big Roller Coaster, Ferris Wheel and Box Ball Alley, etc.

York's Full Concert Band Will Give a Special Select Concert from 4 to 6 in the Evening and Open the Big Dancing Pavilion From 8:30 to 11 at Night

Admission to the Dance---Gentlemen, 75c; Ladies, Free

**At 6. P. M.
Thousands of Ham Sandwiches Will Be Given Away Absolutely Free to Everybody**

The Concert Auxetophone Grand will furnish excellent dance music during the afternoon at the big pavilion. Admission 5c per couple for each dance.

## BASEBALL TOMORROW

AT WHITE CITY PARK.
BELLINGHAM HIGH SCHOOL vs. CUSTER HIGH SCHOOL.
For championship of the county. Game called at 2:30. Admission to ball grounds 25c.

### Plan to Spend Decoration Day at the White City

Admission to grounds 10c, which entitles holder to 10c worth of amusement at any of the devices and also to free ham sandwich. Prices on all amusements have been cut in two; now 5c per trip.

15-Minute Car Service Until Midnight. Whole City Will Close at Noon.

Thousands Will Be at The White City On Memorial Day

The annual Grocers Day picnic at White City is in full swing during a hot summer day in 1909. The White City ball field offered room for all kinds of events including hot air balloon demonstrations. The back fence runs approximately where North Shore drive is now and the wagon ruts running up the hill to the left would eventually become Britton Road. Stenton photo

*Local Grocers Planning Big Picnic*

"Nothing Doing" Sign Will Be
Displayed Next Thursday While
Grocery men And Friends Enjoy
Out on Lake Whatcom

*Another year has rolled around for the Whatcom County Grocers association and next Thursday the "Nothing Doing Today" sign will be displayed upon the doors of all the groceries and butcher shops in town. The clerks and salesmen will throw aside their aprons and be on an equal footing with "The Boss"--- all to spend an enjoyable full days picnic at the White City, on Lake Whatcom. The annual grocer's picnic has become an infallible institution precedented by keen anticipation and perhaps more largely attended than any similar social function. The Grocer's association has proven in year past that it is a good provider, and Miss Elgia M. Stead, secretary of the organization, promises that this year's picnic will eclipse all former efforts.*

*The appointment of the different committees on arrangements has been completed, comprising personnel of almost one hundred business men, so that if influence, affluence and numbers are a criterion all the arrangements will be flawless. The program, comprising no-less than twenty-one athletic and unique novelty events, will of course include afternoon and evening dances at the lake pavilion and a fifteen minute car service will be maintained on the Lake Whatcom line all day long. A caterer named Giles has arranged to prepare a special noon luncheon, to be served on the grounds from 10:00A.M. until evening, so that even the old stand-by picnic basket may be left behind. The association has decided to offer all cash prizes for the program events so that some keen rivalry and competition may be expected.*

*In the order following, the day's events will occur, commencing at 9:30 A.M. and running through on schedule:*

*Baseball game, clerks vs. drivers; baby show; retail clerks race; girls race; grocers race; swinging sack race; girls race; boot race; winners competitive race; girls race; sack race; boys race; fat men's race; delivery men's race; ladies ball throwing contest; straight somersault race; married ladies race potato race; nail driving contest; pie eating contest; package tying contest.*

*York's brass band is to provide the music for the afternoon and evening dances and the grounds will be specially policed to preclude any drinking or rowdyism. The association gives its assurance that it will be a nice clean picnic, and in order to facilitate the travel of those from the south end of the city, special cars will run through from the end of the Happy Valley line, running through to the White City*

Herald- Reveille July 18th 1914

**The York Band in front of the Silver Beach Hotel.**

This is the Silver Beach Hotel in 1910 as seen from the NP trestle. This rare image shows the bear pit sitting just off the beach above the pump house. This pit housed two cub bears that were captured after their mother was shot. They were quite an attraction for the public but in the end they got too big and unruly before winding up sharing the same fate as their mother. The White City Ferris wheel and roller coaster can be seen in the hazy distance.

Another view of the hotel and amusement park from the White City dock. The Ferris wheel can be seen above the ice cream stand. The trolley depot is the dark building on the left. The trolleys came onto the dock to pick up boat passengers from other areas of the lake. Whatcom Museum collection

**Two ladies and a little girl in front of the Silver Beach Hotel around 1910.**
**An afternoon outing has brought these ladies to the Silver Beach Hotel and its commanding view of Lake Whatcom. It was the custom during the early part of the 20th century for men and women to dress sharply for outings and these ladies seem to have done their part in keeping with tradition. Whatcom Museum collection**

**The Lake Whatcom excursion steamer "Elsinore" at the White City dock sometime before the amusement park was built. Another hotel is in the left distance. Whatcom Museum collection**

The "Elsinore" was built near Lake Washington in 1900 and moved by rail to Lake Whatcom around 1903. She ran excursions from Silver Beach down to the southern end of the lake at Park. She made stops at Geneva and Blue Canyon along the way.

In the early days, steamers such as the "Elsinore" would make unscheduled stops along the lake for passengers or mail pick-ups. If someone placed a flag or even a rag on a pole out at the end of their dock, the steamers would pull off their routes and pick up the passengers.

This photo taken from what would become North Shore Drive, shows the Silver Beach Hotel sitting on the northern shore of Lake Whatcom around 1896. It was another decade before it would be refurbished into the White City Amusement Park.
The second Silver Beach School sits on the hill near the tree line. A forest fire destroyed the first school building in 1894. Snags from the fire cover the hillside. The hotel escaped the fire, most likely due to the land around it having been cleared. The area livestock were also spared. The local farmers drove their animals into the lake to save them. Whatcom Museum collection

This 2008 view of the peninsula where White City and the Silver Beach Hotel stood is testament to the fact that the lake is still to be enjoyed and its shores continue to be coveted by those who live along its banks and those who visit from afar.

An overlay of the White City site on a current map.
In 1910, the trolley tracks ended at the White City entrance but the Northern Pacific RR tracks continued past the ice cream parlor over a trestle to the east shore of the lake.
This satellite photo of the Silver Beach neighborhood shows where the White City Amusement Park and the White City ball field locations existed in 1910. The grey line represents the amusement park boundary fence and the black line represents the ball field boundary fence; nothing remains of either complex today. The Silver Beach Market has been identified for reference purposes.

**Photo courtesy of Microsoft Virtual Earth**

# The Mills: Lumber is king…

The first sawmill on Bellingham was put into operation in the late summer of 1853. It was built by Russell Peabody, Henry Roeder, Henry C. Brown, and about a dozen more Europeans and an unknown number of local Natives. Roeder bought out Brown's one-third interest a year later. The mill was an open sided affair with a long look. The frame was covered with hand-split cedar shakes. Power to a single circular saw blade was from belts (most likely leather strips sewn together) driven by a Pelton design water wheel. The source of the water was a ditch (called a millrace) dug to divert water from above the falls at the mouth of Whatcom Creek. The mill was probably capable of producing enough lumber to build a small house about the size of Captain Pickett's in one day, around 4,000 board feet. The main problem was getting logs of the right size that could be man-handled onto the guides going to the saw blade. This mill burned in the early fall of 1873.

The next mill built on Bellingham Bay was the Colony Mill. This mill started production in 1882 on the old Whatcom Falls millsite, and operated through the 1920s. The Mill was capable of turning out 40,000 board feet of lumber a day. At first, it was also powered by the water from the millrace at Whatcom Creek, but later it had a steam boiler which would produce the electricity that the operation demanded. The mill ran in the red until 1885 when Stenger bought it and upgraded it. The Colony that started the mill had money problems as well as a lack of good management. Nelson Bennett bought the mill from Stenger and leased it back. Bennett only wanted the Colony dock for a railroad depot. Bennett also could keep 13th Street from being put through to Holly Street to delay the development of Whatcom as a competitor to his Fairhaven. Bennett failed in both attempts as The Roeder/Pettibone forces joined with the Stangroom/Cornwall interests to create the city of New Whatcom.

The third mill on the bay was the Red Mill, owned and operated by Edward Eldridge and Erastus Bartlett. Bartlett was a silent partner in the deal. Being somewhat reclusive, Bartlett believed in the powers of spiritualism and would only make a deal if he believed that the spirits had given their blessing. This mill, built in 1883 and located at present-day Boulevard Park, was also a small mill. In the photo of Dan Harris standing in his rowboat at Fairhaven, taken around 1888, The Red Mill can be seen in the background. The Red Mill was bought and expanded by E. K. Wood and his family.

Another earlier mill was the Globe Mill, run by S. D. Wyman. The mill sat out on the mud flats and was the first mill not serviced by ships. By the time this mill was in operation, the train tracks were close enough that a spur was built into the mill. This mill would become a part of the much larger Morrison Mill.

These mills were small for several reasons. The market demand was only along the west coast and there were many mills in competition. Larger mills required more logs and the logging techniques in the 1880s, especially in and around Bellingham Bay, were quite limited in nature. Trees of the proper size would be cut down and dragged along skid roads by teams of oxen or horses, then rolled into a waterway or the bay, then boomed together and then towed to the mill. Toothed chains drug the logs up into the mill, where they were cut either by a single circular saw blade or by several blades fastened together. Early lumber was most likely non-dimensional as the logs were usually moved by hand and close measurement was done by eyeing the piece as it approached the saw. Another belt drove a planner to smooth the lumber and make it more dimensional. By 1880, with the onset of the steam donkey and its applications in the woods and the mills, more timber could be cut faster and loaded onto railroad flat cars, then shipped to a mill that had more power to move the logs into the mill. Improved machinery meant that the same dimension could be cut every time. Only the length would differ. By running multiple saws, different dimensions could be cut at the same time, so many of the mills became quite large in order to meet all of the dimensions demanded by the lumber buyers.

**A 11 foot diameter fir log, destined for a Bellingham Bay mill, c1908**

The Bellingham Bay Improvement Company Mill started operations during the boom year of 1890. Stangroom also put in a larger power plant that generated surplus DC electrical power to the cities of New Whatcom and Whatcom. Arc light lamps were installed on the streets and in many of the shops, competing with the coal gas production plant above the present-day Boulevard Park. When the streets were being laid out and cleared in town, the water, sewer, and gas mains also went in.

The BBIC soon grew into one of the larger mills on the waterfront. The mill produced an average of 50,000 board feet of lumber a day. The water was deep enough that ocean-going ships could load and unload at the BBIC dock. The mill burned down in 1898 but was rebuilt. Bloedel and Donovan bought the mill in 1913.

**Peter Hegg took this photo of a fir log in 1905. Peter worked with his brother, E. A. Hegg, the famous Alaska-Yukon gold rush photographer.**

Peter Larson was the promoter of his mill on the north end of Lake Whatcom in 1898. By 1907, when Larson died, the Larson Mill was so large that it had its own town. Larson had formed the Lake Whatcom Logging Company with his partners Bloedel and Donovan. They cut timber and hauled it across the lake to the Geneva Mill, which they later bought. Julius H. Bloedel and John J. Donovan had met in Fairhaven where Donovan was the superintendent for the Fairhaven and Southern Railroad. Bloedel and James Wardner had organized the Samish Lake Logging Company. In 1891, Bloedel became the Vice-President of the First National Bank of Fairhaven, and later in 1893, the President.

In 1891, Donovan built the Bellingham Bay and Eastern Railroad around Lake Whatcom to Wickersham to connect with the NP line. By 1898, Donovan was hired to be the chief engineer for the BB&BC Railroad. His primary job was to haul logs to the mills. That same year, Donovan, Bloedel, and Peter Larson formed the Lake Whatcom Logging Company. In 1902 they bought the McCue and Hastings mills on the lake. In 1906, the Larson Mill was built next to the McCue Mill. These became the A and B mills, with over 500 men working in the mills.

**Idealized drawing of the Larson Mill at Lake Whatcom about 1905.**

**Aerial view of the Bloedel Donovan Mill at Lake Whatcom, 1928. In 1907, Peter Larson died, and his business partners assumed control of the company. The company was renamed in 1913, the same year that Bloedel and Donovan bought the BBIC millsite on the bay and rebuilt it as the Bloedel Donovan Cargo Mill.**

By 1915, Bloedel and Donovan owned several large lumber yards and a fleet of ships carrying lumber to southern ports and to ports in Asia. The company had offices in Los Angeles, New York, and Chicago, and was headquartered in Seattle, Bloedel's home city. In 1925, a box mill was built at the foot of Cornwall Avenue. The box mill office is still standing.

For some time up through the 1940s, the Bloedel Donovan Mill was one of the largest in the world. During WWII, the box mill produced wood crates and boxes, using about 140,000 board feet of lumber in a 24 hour period.

By 1945, due to decreases in available timber coupled with the age of the mills and equipment, Bloedel and Donovan started down-sizing. The timber property was sold to Raynier and the waterfront mill was sold to the Port of Bellingham. Liquidation was completed in 1948 with the B mill site on the lake donated to the Bellingham Parks department. The A mill continued to operate until 1957, when it also shut down. That property is now the site of the Millwheel Village. In all of the years that the company operated, it processed over 5 billion board feet of lumber.

The Columbia Valley Lumber Company started up in 1911. A small mill, it cut lumber for the local market. It sold off the mill in 1945 but continued to sell lumber products through the 1980s.

The Colony Mill was leased by George Loggie in 1885 and by 1905, Loggie had expanded his operation into the largest shingle mill in the world. The Loggie Mill was so large that almost the whole end of the bay was filled with log booms destined to be cut or split in the mill.

**The Loggie mill, about 1905, is seen in this stereoview.**

Howard Buswell Photograph #1433
Center for Pacific Northwest Studies
Western Washington University
Bellingham WA 98225-9123

**The Colony Mill continued to be used for lumber cutting and storage until the late 1920s. It was used for a time by the Bellingham Sash and Door Company. About this time, Bellingham Sash and Door bought the Holly Street end of the block between C Street and the old Colony Dock and turned it into their offices and showroom. The old Whatcom Mill office is on the bluff and the Colony Mill office sits where the old mill was located at the mouth of the creek.**

**Bellingham Sash and Door later became Builders Alliance and moved out to the Hannegan Road. The store building was taken over by the Re-store. In 2008, the store is empty. The Colony dock gradually disappeared, mostly used for securing log booms until the big mills shut down and the pilings were knocked down. The mill also gradually disappeared. Today the site is completely filled in. The pilings at the mouth of Whatcom Creek are the remnants of the Colony Mill dock.**

In 1908, the Loggie Mill dominated the north side of Bellingham Bay.

The Morrison Mill was owned by the six Morrison brothers. There were Morrison Mills at Blaine and Ferndale. The Morrison Mill site was eventually filled in and the property became the site of Puget Sound Pulp and Timber, which in turn became Georgia Pacific.

The Loggie Mill was the largest shingle mill in the world in 1908 but it too would eventually shut down in 1940, mostly due to the lack of timber. The mills along Bellingham Bay and Lake Whatcom cut an average of about 5 million board feet per week. By 1937, the timber that was supposed to supply these mills for centuries had been cut. It took about 200,000 trees a year to support the mills.

There are three pile drivers tied up to the Morrison Mill pier. These were used to set pilings for the log booms located to the right.

The old Colony Dock runs across the front of the Loggie Mill. Whatcom Museum collection

The E. K. Wood Mill was another large mill on Bellingham Bay. Edwin Kleber Wood was born in 1840 in New York State and fought in the Civil War, then became a teacher. While on a trip to the mid-west after the war, Wood was persuaded to move to Michigan and get into logging. After buying a mill, Wood and his brother-in-law, Clarence Thayer, built the business into one of the largest lumber producers in the state.

In 1888, Thayer moved to San Francisco and opened an office under the name of the E. K. Wood Lumber Company. The business partners started up several mills on the west coast, six in California and the one in Bellingham. Edwin's son Fred ran the Bellingham Mill, shipping lumber all along the west coast and to the orient.

Galen Biery papers and photographs #107
Center for Pacific Northwest Studies
Western Washington University
Bellingham, WA 98225

**The E. K. Wood Mill loading dock with nine schooners loading lumber. The NP tracks were out on pilings. The GN tracks ran on the shore. An E. K. Wood 3 masted schooner, the "C. Thayer", has been restored and can be seen tied up at San Francisco.**

Wood bought the old Eldridge-Bartlett mill in 1900 and within a few years, the mill was producing over 160,000 board feet of lumber a day. Over 150 men were employed at the mill until it burned in September of 1925. The mill was never rebuilt. The coffee shop at Boulevard Park is an old restored E. K. Wood Mill building.

In 1897, Michael Earles and Ed Cleary built a mill in the small bay just east of the mouth of Padden Creek in Fairhaven. By 1900, it was the Puget Sound Mill. That year, the Puget Sound Mill processed almost 20 million board feet of lumber and 135 million cedar shingles, making it the largest sawmill in the world at the time. In 1905, five of the ten largest saw mills in the world were located at Bellingham. In 1910, the Puget Sound Mill could produce a million board feet of lumber in 3 days.

**The Puget Sound Mill, 1910. The Wardner home can be seen on the horizon above downtown Fairhaven district. Oakes photo**

By 1930, the glory years of the local saw mills were over. The production of the mills in Bellingham had peaked and was starting to decline. Logging railroads criss-crossed the forests, hauling the huge sections of old growth back toward the bay, much of it one log on one railroad car. Such sustained cutting meant that someday the timber would run out, and the second growth trees weren't large enough to make up the volume. By the time of the great depression, most of the large mills had shut down, and the lack of money and demand, coupled with a decrease in easily accessed large trees in the area of Bellingham, caused many of the mill owners to move to areas with more accessible trees and newer mill equipment. Transportation also played a part in the closing of the mills along the bay. The fact was that a saw mill didn't need to be near water any more. New logging techniques, the rapid advance of logging trucks and updated equipment in mills meant that a mill could be set up closer to a good source of timber. By the mid 1960s, Bloedel mills were operating in Canada where large logs could still be cut. The Summit Mill in Darrington, Washington, could cut one million board feet of lumber in one day with modern machinery. Shipping lumber overseas was out, shipping logs overseas was in. Today, most of the lumber used for construction in Bellingham is now cut in Canada.

"From Loop's ranch, Forks, Whatcom Co. Washington
The Tree was 465 ft high, 220 ft to the first limb. 33 ft, 11 inches in circumference at the base. If sawed into lumber would make 96345 feet. Would build 8 cottages 2 stories 7 rooms each. The tree is about 480 years old according to the rings. If sawed into inch square strips, would fill 10 ordinary cars. The strips would reach from Whatcom to China." Lithograph from the magazine "The Coast" June, 1906.

# State Street

**This sketch of Sehome is the earliest known picture of the town. Supposedly drawn by Captain George Pickett, the drawing is a layout of the town, with numbers describing the buildings.**

Long considered the main street of Bellingham, the State Street of today is just a shadow of itself. Pickett's Military Road was the first such roadway in the area, running along the top of the bluff, winding around the huge stumps left by the men cutting and splitting the timbers for the Sehome Coal mine tunnels that lay beneath their feet. In 1854 the mine entrance was at the base of the bluff along the beach. The mine buildings and supporting structures sat above the entrance on the nearest level ground in the area. A narrow strip of rocky beach separated the mudflats from the bottom slope of the bluff. A steep path led to the top of the hill. Later, the mine entrance was moved to the top of the bluff. This upper entrance was along a bench that ran just below the top of the bluff. The bench sloped downhill and southward toward the water's edge, forming a nice incline that was used to access the first dock built to load the coal onto the ships that hauled it to San Francisco.

The town first had a couple of shacks to house the mine equipment and a hotel to house the workers. Other nearby buildings included a couple of farmhouses and the mine office, general store, and a saloon of course.

The store and saloon were owned by the mine owners. Later, in the 1870s, a home was built for the mine manager. This home was the finest dwelling on the bay for a number of years. The land was cleared around the dwelling and a white picket fence surrounded the house and an orchard was planted on the grounds by an early pioneer, John Bennett, one of the more famous individuals in the area (John Bennett was a horticulturist who developed several new varieties of plants, including the Bennett pear).

Galen Biery papers and photographs #1454
Center for Pacific Northwest Studies
Western Washington University
Bellingham, WA 98225

**This photo is of the Orchard Terrace, built in the 1870s for the manager of the Bellingham Bay Coal Company. After the mine closed in 1878, the home was used as the office of the Bellingham Bay Improvement Company and the Bellingham Bay and British Columbia Railroad Company. The BBIC and the BB&BC were controlled by Pierre Cornwall.**

**The brightly colored buildings fronting Forest Street are the Orchard Terrace Apartments. The photo was taken from the west side of State Street between Rose and Laurel Streets in 2008.**

The mine was named the Sehome Mine after the first mine manager's father-in-law, a minor chief of the S'Klallams. The little village that grew around the mine was also called Sehome. Eventually the mine became the largest employer north of Seattle, and the village became the largest town in the area.

There aren't any early photographs of the area. Photographers traveled from place to place carrying their equipment with them. Early cameras and the processing equipment necessary to produce the pictures were bulky and heavy. Most photographers used wagons to carry their studios around, and since there wasn't any road into the area, there weren't any photographers. The earliest recorded instance of a photographer at Bellingham Bay was at the Fourth of July event that took place in Sehome in 1873. This photographer arrived by boat. It was noted in the Bellingham Bay Mail that a traveling photographer, was in town to take pictures of the celebration and of a wedding, and that individual sittings were available.
Prior to this, there are two sketches of the town of Sehome, the first done by Captain Pickett in 1959 and the second done by Edmund T. Coleman for the November 1869 article in Harper's on the climb to the summit of Mt. Baker.
A later photograph taken in 1884 of the buildings along Division Street in Whatcom shows Sehome across the bay. About 25 buildings are aligned along the cow path known as Elk Street. This photo also shows the grade of the Bellingham Bay and British Columbia RR. extending downward toward the Sehome Dock which is out of the right side of the picture.
A E Hegg took the 1888 photograph of Sehome looking north from approximately the present-day location of the VFW on State Street. This photograph may have been taken as early as 1886.

**A view of Sehome taken sometime between 1886 and 1888.**

**A detail from the previous photograph. The first Sehome school is on the left side by itself. The second and third openings into the Sehome Coal Mine are to the left of the railroad tracks at the edge of the bluff. The railroad tracks come from the Sehome dock out the photo to the left toward the upper middle of the photo. The BB&BC tracks ended at present-day Chestnut Street, as do the row of buildings along Elk (renamed State Street in 1927). The railroad had no cars or locomotives at this time. The fence on the right side of the street surrounds the Orchard Terrace, office of the BB&BC in 1883, and in 1889, the BBIC. The building north of the fence on the right side is the Keystone (Sehome) Hotel, moved from its original site which would have been in the middle of the street almost in front of the Orchard Terrace. The Morse Hardware store is almost directly across from the Keystone Hotel.**

Another photo taken in 1888 from the Whatcom side with Sehome across the bay in the background shows very little south of Berry Street, but does verify the layout of the buildings along Elk Street in the vicinity of the Morse Hardware store.

During the frenzied activity associated with the coming of the railroads in 1889, Elk Street construction matched the activity everywhere else along the bay. Stores, hotels, boarding houses, restaurants, and shops were built as fast as the workers could put them together. Sehome doubled in size in just a few months. Workers were housed in tents and made premium wages, especially if they were experienced. By late 1891, Sehome, (re-named New Whatcom by the BBIC, the major developer), had merged with the city of Whatcom to form the much larger city of New Whatcom.

The main business section of Elk Street was lined with new buildings by the summer of 1889. the Sehome Hotel, completed in 1888, with its flag flying high didn't even have a side walk yet. The Sehome Hotel was on the corner of Berry and Elk.

The crews were still laying planks on the street and the trolley tracks weren't laid yet. The picket fence is around the Orchard Terrace (BBIC office) property while the white wood rail stairs are going up to the entrance of the Keystone Hotel. Rose Street would eventually run to the left between Orchard Terrace and the Keystone Hotel.

The Keystone, originally named the Sehome Hotel in the 1850s, had been moved from its original location across from the Orchard Terrace. Whatcom Museum collection

In this 2008 photo taken from the corner of Laurel and State Street, nothing remains of the 1889 buildings on either side of the street. The Jones and Carlyon Real Estate investment company building is now the Toth Upholstery shop. The small corner overhanging "tower" burned a few years ago but the owner decided to keep the original look and rebuilt the overhang. Jones and Carlyon built hotels to attract newcomers to the area. They developed the Silver Beach area and the Silver Beach Hotel. They also built the Grand Central Hotel which was at Holly and Forest. They developed hundreds of lots in Whatcom and New Whatcom.

Dobbs and Fleming were photographers in Sehome. Beverly Dobbs (Beverly was a man's name in the 1890s) went to the Yukon in the late 1890s and photographed the gold rush there. Dobbs also photographed many of the scenes and people of the Yukon and Alaska.

Sehome was experiencing rapid growth in 1889 when this photo was taken. The right-of-way for Forest Street won't be completed for around 20 more years. The stores on the left are along Elk Street. The house with the white picket fence is the Orchard Terrace, office of the BBIC. Soon the Pike Block and Sunset Block would also grace the city skyline. By 1891, all of the vacant lots were filled with shops and homes. Whatcom Museum collection

In 1890 Dozens of shops lined both sides of Elk Street. Most were completed even before the street was. Stumps can still be seen in this photo. Dynamite was used to clear the streets of sandstone and stumps, creating a large demand for the replacement of broken windows about once a week.

The major business section for the new city was at the intersection of Elk and Holly Streets. The more prominent businessmen had offices in the new buildings on two of the four corners. Two of these were magnificent stone and brick structures and the other two corners had wooden structures. These wood buildings were thrown up in the rush of 1889 and were replaced by 1908.

Major construction was also taking place along 13th Street between the Whatcom Creek waterway and Broadway. Most of these buildings were built of wood, with the exception of the Roth Block which was brick and sandstone. The larger buildings along 13th were small shops and hotels. In comparison, the buildings along Elk Street housed professional offices and those shops frequented by businessmen. The shops extended south on both sides along Elk Street from Magnolia Street to Cedar Street. Many of these buildings were built of brick and some stone.

**The Pike Block was completed in 1891 and served as the main office of the Bellingham Bay National Bank, as well as a number of investment firms, real estate offices, and law offices.**
**In 1912, the building was owned by the Puget Sound Traction and Light Company. In this 1915 photo, the Interurban office occupies the basement floor. The Interurban started up in 1912. Puget Sound Traction and Light, all of the trolley system, and all of the electric generating plants were owned by Stone and Webster, a very large investment firm that specialized in electrical production and use. The building was abandoned in 1928 when Puget Sound Power moved north to the SW corner of State and Magnolia Streets. The Pike block stayed empty due to damage caused by the settling of the tunnels of the Sehome Coal Mine. The building was demolished in 1938 and is now the site of the Saturna office building.**
**Whatcom Museum collection**

Elk Street was the main thoroughfare for several years. Gradually the main business center shifted to the area bounded by Railroad Avenue, Chestnut Street, Prospect Street, and Grand Street. This shift was completed when the Bellingham National Bank was completed in 1912. By 1914, this central district contained the major lodging, entertainment, and business blocks in the city. Elk Street gradually settled into a middle-aged genteel but shabby existence. Elk Street became more of a working class area, with boarding houses next to automobile shops, small cafes, and saloons.

Over time, many of the older buildings along Elk Street, especially the wood framed ones, burned. Most of these were not replaced, leaving gaps in the rows of shops and hotels. The biggest change came when the Pike Block on the NE corner of Elk and Holly was abandoned due to the danger of collapse and a later fire. By this time, in 1930, the Depression was in full force, and the building would sit there for seven more years, a testament to the bad times, a broken monument to the glory years of Elk Street.

In 1967, the Exchange Block, now the YMCA, suffered the indignity of a very ugly "upgrade" with the aluminum "modern" covering. In June of 1969, the Alaska building, on the SW corner of State and Holly, burned. In 1971, the Sunset Block was torn down. The McLeod Block burned in 1974.

BNB built the city's largest drive-in bank on the old Alaska Block site in 1979. A big event at first, the novelty gradually wore off and eventually the branch closed and was torn down.

Surprisingly, State Street never became a slum area containing flop houses and other lowly dives such as happened to lower Fairhaven. Perhaps it was due to the proximity of the homes of the shopkeepers and businessmen that lined the streets on the hill above. The main business center was only a block away and this too, may have kept the area more upscale. Also, many of the remaining businesses along State Street were family owned. However, strange neighbors have lined the street in the last few decades. Such businesses as the triple X rated Green Apple Movie Theater, the "world famous" Up and Up Tavern, and the 3B tavern, have rubbed elbows with the original Shakey's Pizza House, the largest drive-in bank in Bellingham, George Buchinoff's Bellingham Upholstery Shop, and the prestigious Masonic Temple.

Today, State Street has been revitalized, with the opening of upscale shops and a small resurgence of the professional businesses. The YMCA finally realized their mistake and have done an excellent job of restoring the front of their building. The Laube Hotel is undergoing a transformation that will retain some of the old elegance. The Key Bank is preparing to fill in the gap left by the McLeod and Alaska Block destruction and the demolition of the drive-in bank that later occupied the corner. Soon someone will start to renovate the old Dahlquist Grocery building and complete the transformation of the area. Although State Street may never regain the glory days of its beginning, it is still one of the main streets of Bellingham, a place of comfort and delight.

A lithograph of Elk Street in 1907. Construction debris is piled in the street from the Exchange Building site. The McLeod Block is on the right, then the Pantage's Theater, then a small shop, and finally the Daylight Block. The picture was taken from the corner of State and Holly. The Alaska Block would be built in 1909 on the corner out of the photo to the right.

In the 2008 photo below, the only surviving structure is the Daylight Block. The Herald Building is south on the next block. The vacant lot is being readied for a new Key Bank building that replaces the old BNB/Key Bank drive-up bank.

In 1904, the Laube Block contained the Laube Hotel and Restaurant, and the adjoining Windsor Hotel. The hotel taxi sat in front posing for the cameraman. For a while the Laube was the best hotel in town. It soon would be outdone by the Byron on Dock (now Cornwall) Street.

The 2008 photo shows the Laube nearing the end of a complete remodel. Placed on the State register a few years ago, the building exterior is much the same as the original. The hotel has been redone as a low income apartment with commercial shops on the street level. The Color Pot store has replaced the old Thomas Slade Real Estate building.

Galen Biery photograph #672, Center for Pacific NW Studies

**J. P. DeMattos' Sunset block was completed at the height of the 1890 boom, and served as one of the anchor blocks for the professional center of Whatcom, and later Bellingham, for many years. When DeMattos had some financial difficulties, the BBIC took over the building. The BBIC remodelled the building in 1907, adding an upper floor. The main corner entrance led into the Scandinavian American Bank. The entrance to the upstairs was to the right, and the upper offices held lawyers, dentists, and other professionals. Toward the end of its life, the building held the Dream Theater, a pool hall and other more non-professional occupants. The building was demolished in 1971, and the space sat vacant for about 20 years before the Horizon Bank built a branch office on the property. In the 2008 photo, he building in the rear is the south wall of the Dahlquist Grocery Company block.**

The William Tell saloon was opened in 1902 by Betschart and Steiner in the new Betschart Building. The William Tell Saloon was a popular hangout until prohibition was voted in by Bellingham citizens in 1911. The saloons in town either served local beer from Jacob Beck's Whatcom Brewery or the 3B Brewery run by Leopold Schmidt. According to the signs, 3B beer was sold by the William Tell.

The William Tell Hotel occupied the building's upper floor until around 1924, when it became the Elk Hotel. From about 1912 until 1930, the bottom floor was vacant. The upper floor was the Irving Hotel in the late 1920s and early 1930s. In 1930, Tegenfeldt and Farquharson had their plumbing and heating shop in the main floor shop, then the downstairs was empty until 1935, when Clark Plumbing and Heating was on the main floor. In 1945, the main floor was an office of the Model Truck and Storage Company. The Cozy Apartments were upstairs. In 1948, the Bellingham Labor Council was on the main floor. In 1959, Technocracy, Inc was on the main floor and a dance studio was on the upper floor.

In 1975, Tom's Beaver Inn moved into the main floor and has been there ever since. The upstairs units are private apartments.

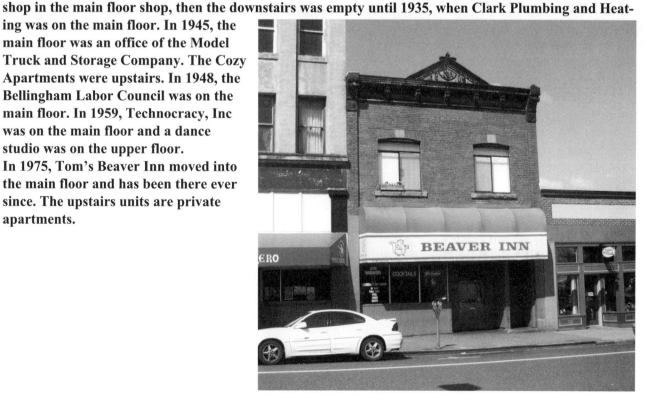

**In 1975, a spectacular blaze was set by an occupant of the Antler Hotel on the upper floor of the Dahlquist Block. The fire gutted the upper floors. The Dahlquist Block was built in 1904 and had the Mullin Hotel on the upper floors. Dahlquist, a former employee with the Bellingham Bay Grocers wholesale outlet, went into competition with his former employer. The Dahlquist was a grand building, built with re-enforced concrete. Dahlquist also had a retail outlet. At the time of the fire, the property was owned by the Chin family. Chin moved the New China café into the ground floor from its former location on Cornwall, across from the Leopold Hotel. Tom's Beaver Inn was also in the building before moving into the Betschart building next door.**
**The only business operating in the building today is the Rogue Hero Tavern. After the fire, the upper floors and roof were rebuilt but nothing else has been done to make the building usable. In 2008, the Rogue Hero is remodeling the old New China cafe for an expansion.**
Whatcom Museum collection

In this 2008 photo, the Dahlquist name can be seen between the corbels along the roof. The faded name on the front is "Hotel Mullin".

In 1928, Puget Sound Power and Light moved from the Pike Block on the NE corner of State and Holly Streets into their new building on the SW corner of Magnolia and Holly Streets. This photo, taken about 1930, shows the fine architecture of the building. At this time, Puget Sound Power and Light also owned the North Coast Transportation Company. In the late 1880s, Stone and Webster, two electrical engineers, decided to pool their resources and started an investment group that specialized in all things dealing with electricity. By 1912, the company owned hundreds of small power plants and power utilities across the country.

They built the power plant on York Street to run the trolley system that they owned. A few years later, they bought the power plant at Nooksack Falls to supply the growing demand for electricity. The BBIC had built the stucture but had so many problems getting the plant to work that they gladly sold it to Stone and Webster. The only competition in Whatcom County was the generator at the BBIC mill. Stone and Webster favored alternating current while the BBIC mill put out direct current. The main problem with DC power was the need for an elaborate network of boosters. The longest distance that could be covered with DC power without a booster was about 5 miles. Alternating current could go for many miles without a booster. In 1912, Stone and Webster created the Interurban that ran from Bellingham to Mount Vernon. By 1925, the interurban was losing money in competition with the automobile. To counter the problem with the frequent shutdowns of the interurban, the company started the North Coast bus line from Bellingham to Mount Vernon along the main highway of the time, Chuckanut Drive. In 1928, the interurban quit carrying passengers, and the bus depot was opened in the new building. In the 1930s, Puget Sound Power had to sell off the bus service due to a violation of the laws dealing with monopolies. The Greyhound Bus line was formed and split off, but continued to use the building until the late 1990s when the new bus terminal opened in the old PAF office building. Shortly after, Puget Sound opened a new administrative office near Seattle and in 2008 the building is being remodeled for a new tenant.

Galen Biery papers and photographs #902
Center for Pacific Northwest Studies
Western Washington University
Bellingham, WA 98225

**In 1908, the Jones and Carlyon Real Estate office was one of the finer buildings along Elk Street at Laurel. The north end of the building was home to the Bellingham Bay Bottling Company.**
**The vacant lot up the block had housed the Keystone Hotel which was torn down in 1906. The block with its onion dome turret was the office for the Slade Real Estate Company.**

**In 2008, the Jones and Carlyon block has had two garage doors added to the front for access to the upholstery shop. The Slade Block is gone, victim of a fire in 1958.**

**The local National Guard is marching in a parade on Elk Street in 1904. The stores take up the SW corner of Chestnut and Elk Streets.**

**The Herald Building, completed in 1927, takes up the corner in 2008. It was the tallest building in Bellingham until the Bellingham Hotel was completed two years later.**

Galen Biery papers and photographs #540
Center for Pacific Northwest Studies
Western Washington University
Bellingham, WA 98225

**On November 10, 1910, the cornerstone for the Bellingham Armory was laid.**

**This 2008 photo shows one of the problems in doing a then and now comparison; trees.
The homes on the hillside above State Street are all still there, but the Assumption Catholic Church is gone.**

Sitting up on the hill above Bellingham Bay, the armory was the result of years of political maneuvering and hundreds of newspaper articles. Bellingham was the home of Company F of the First Infantry Regiment of the National Guard. Formed in New Whatcom in 1890 by Colonel John J. Weisenburger, the Guard was the pride and joy of the city. The Guard marched in every parade and participated in WWI and WWII. Due to the problems with weather, the Guard held a lot of drills and meetings in various buildings in the early years. Finally, the guard had an office attached to the Fairyland Skating Rink on the NE corner of Holly and Garden Streets and practiced on the skating rink floor whenever they could get the space.

Eventually, the Guard was granted a sum of $75,000 for the construction of their own building. The walls were built with re-enforced concrete and faced with Chuckanut Sandstone. The architect decided on a castle look and crenellations were placed along the top. A curved roof sat over the drill floor. This floor had a balcony that ran around the room. The balcony had offices and classrooms. The main, or middle floor, was the drill area. The bottom floor had a large door to allow for big equipment. There also was a small arms indoor firing range on the bottom floor. The building was also used for such diverse programs as school and public dances and graduations, and other presentations. The guard moved out in 1953 and the building was then used for roller skating, and even had a ring set up for boxing and wrestling matches.

In 1972, the building was sold for one dollar to Western Washington University to be used for storage. It also continued to be used for a roller skating rink but water damage to the floor eventually made the building unfit for skating. The roof has been repaired several times but needs to be entirely replaced.

Today the building is still used for storage by WWU. However, the upper floor has been badly neglected and the skylight has been broken out, exposing the fine wood floor and upper balcony to the elements. WWU has committed to refurbishing the structure as time and money allows. The building is presently on the Washington Trust for Historical Preservation's list of most endangered sites.

**A view of the armory near the end of construction. Except for the trees, the building looks the same today as it did 98 years ago.**

The Armory in 2008. Even the telephone pole is in the same location.

The Assumption Catholic Church was dedicated in 1889 on Elk Street at the top of the hill. It overlooked the bay and is quite prominent in any of the photos taken of Sehome Hill during that time. Stenton photo

After the breakaway of the southside parish in 1905, the church location was at the extreme south end of the main Bellingham area. About this time, land was purchased for the construction of the Assumption School on Dock Street (Cornwall Avenue). The school was completed in 1913 but WWI delayed the dedication of the new parish sanctuary until October of 1921. The rectory sits to the left in the photo.
The pews and alter were moved to the new sanctuary and the old church was used for storage. It was demolished around 1930.

In 2008, the church is gone but the rectory still stands and is a private residence.

**The Saint Joseph Hospital on State Street, 1907**

In the 1890s, the cities on Bellingham Bay needed a hospital so they advertised for one. They got two; St. Lukes and St. Joseph. In 1891, The Sisters of St. Joseph arrived and set up a hospital in Fairhaven. Originally in a downtown Fairhaven building, the community leaders gave the hospital land to build a larger hospital on 17th Street. In 1901, the Sisters decided to centralize their location and had a hospital built on State Street midway between Fairhaven and downtown Bellingham, near the Assumption Church. As the community grew, so did the hospital.

**In this 1921 photo of the docks at the Bloedel Mill, Saint Joseph Hospital can be seen on the side of Sehome Hill above the steam plume at the mill. Jukes photo**

By 1907, the population of Bellingham had almost doubled. A large expansion of the hospital was completed. The stone faced structures along the sidewalk contained the steam plant. Large metal doors enclosed the coal bunker for the boiler. A driveway was built on the north side to accommodate ambulances. The workmens' shack sits on the sidewalk. Note the scaffolding and temporary boards in the window frames. Stenton photo

The hospital was still undergoing more expansion in 1911. Note the pile of sandstone in the yard below the original building.

Saint Joseph Hospital in 1930. The auto belonged to the photographer. Another expansion was completed in 1927. Jukes photo

**By 1950, another whole section had been added. The hospital was also a teaching hospital for nurses. Saint Joseph was now several times larger than its rival, St. Luke.**
**Both hospitals now served all of Whatcom County. Most of the private hospitals had closed in the previous decades. Banks photo**

By the 1960s, the older buildings had serious problems and needed to be totally upgraded or replaced. The location was no longer a problem with the advances in ambulance service and the formation of the first fire department aid cars. The decision was made to build a new hospital, and in 1961, 65 acres were purchased at the north end of Ellis Street. In 1966, the new hospital at the north end of Bellingham opened, and shortly after, much of the old hospital was torn down. A portion of the newer structures were converted into apartments and condominiums.
In 1989, St. Joseph's became a Peace Health property.

**2008 photo. The last expansion built in 1949 was converted into apartments.**

The original hospital buildings are gone, replaced by the sterile face of the newer South Hill Apartments. The rough sandstone remnants of the old steam plant clash in vivid contrast to the flat surfaces of the newer building.

## SOME WHATCOM SCHOOLS

Galen Biery papers and photographs #1543
Center for Pacific Northwest Studies
Western Washington University
Bellingham, WA 98225

**Whatcom schools on Dupont Street, c1905. The first Roeder Grade School was built in 1884 and the Central High School in 1889. The high school was the first one in the county. By 1905, the city had outgrown both buildings, and in 1903, the North Side High School was completed on Halleck Street.**

**This rare photo of Roeder school with its windows yet to be installed, was taken just before it's completion in 1908. The two wings are located over the approximate footprints of the two old wooden Central elementary and high school buildings that had previously occupied the site.**

The building sits on property that was donated by Henry Roeder and cost between $45,000 and $50,000 dollars to build. The building was formally dedicated in 1909 with Mrs. Lottie Roth, daughter of Henry and Elizabeth Roeder, giving the keynote speech. She presented the school with life-size pictures of her father and mother. The school's student body ranged from 1st through 8th grades. An emphasis was placed towards the manual arts in response to the fact that 80% of the students would be supporting themselves with their hands as adults.

**The Roeder School in 1911. Jim Doidge photo**

In 1927 Roeder became the first Junior high school in Bellingham with grades 7th through 9th. In 1937, with Bellingham High School opening, Whatcom High became the new junior high school along with a new Fairhaven Junior High School. Roeder was subsequently turned into a kindergarten through 6th grade school, and later became the Bellingham School District administration office.

Overcrowded, lacking in up-to-date equipment and declared to be "unsanitary" by the city board of health, the North Side High School (Whatcom) in 1913 was at the forefront of the school board request for a new central high school.

**This photo of the school shows the original roof line. The building was constructed in 1903 as posted on the gable, and was significantly expanded in 1916. During the expansion, the pitched roof was replaced with a flat design and the building was extended to nearly a block in length. Possibly to save money, the original front doorway was left in place and remains part of the exterior to this day.**

**North Side High School in 1912. The Gym and classrooms for the industrial arts was connected to the rear of the main building. Halleck and F Streets were just dirt strips. F Street runs across the top of the photo. The teacher's residence was connected by a paved path and faced Irving Street which was a main thouroghfare at the time. Detail from a Sandison Balloon photo**

With available building land near Sehome Hill at Forest and Cedar Streets, a school bond to cover the $225,000 construction cost was put forth before the voters. The school board noted that the existing building was really designed as a grade school and could be easily re-configured for that use. The voters were unmoved and the bond was defeated.

After the defeat by the voters, a much cheaper solution to the problem had to be found. It was decided to enlarge the existing school by constructing an addition all the way to F Street, tripling the size of the school. The old "unsanitary" building was never torn down but actually incorporated into the new structure.

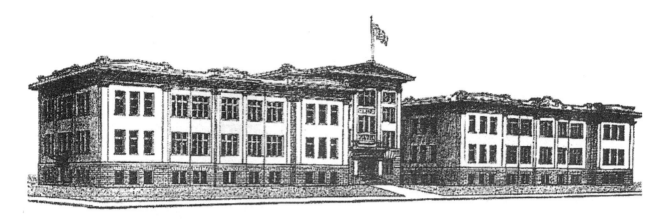

**An architect's drawing of the proposed addition for the North Side High School.**

During construction, the students continued to use the old building. In 1916, the new portion was ready for occupancy and with much fan fare the students marched from the front door of the old building to the entrance of the new building The North Side High School was renamed Whatcom High. The building housed the high school until the new Bellingham High School was built in 1937. After that time it became known as Whatcom Junior High with its academic classes ranging from seventh through the ninth grade. In 1967 it changed its class range from sixth through eighth grades when it was reassigned as a middle school and continues in that capacity today. The word Junior was added above the entrance to reflect the change to a Junior High School, and then both Junior and High were removed when the building became a middle school.

**Whatcom High School, around 1930. Clyde Banks photo**

**The old entrance to the North Side High School is still outlined on the building but the doors are no longer in place.**

The Whatcom Middle School is the oldest school building in use by the students of Bellingham. Solidly constructed, it has out-lasted other school buildings that have been built since.

If you walk the basement of Whatcom, you can still see where the old school building stopped and the 1916 addition began; look for the brick walls.

**The tree shrouded building still stands strong in 2008.**

## Henry Roeder's Elmheim

Henry and Elizabeth Roeder spent over forty years on Bellingham Bay; working, scrimping, and saving their hard-earned money. By 1890, the Roeders were perched at the social summit of the community. Elizabeth was a revered member of upper society, and being a founding pioneer and civic leader, found herself working in the few places that women of her time were allowed to work. She concentrated most of her energies on the church and miscellaneous women's organizations.

Henry was a leader in the community and held a position in the upper circles of men's organizations and business activities. By 1890 he had retired as the major partner in the Chuckanut Sandstone quarry and the president of the First National Bank.

In the early years, the Roeders moved from a little log cabin near the mouth of Whatcom Creek to a substantial home along the bluff. Natural disasters took their toll on the house. Forest fires that swept through parts of the business district of Whatcom consumed the Roeder home twice.

The first house that the Roeders built on the bluff had the look of the standard farmhouse of the time; simple in design, built for comfort and yet it must have retained some exceptional qualities as is evident to the fact that the Roeders hosted a few of the rare societal events of the time. It was also known that they would, on occasion, board newcomers to the area until they had a chance to settle into a home of their own.

The second home was built to a more sociable style. It boasted a substantial array of amenities including gingerbread detailing on the exterior.

Henry was a member of the territorial legislature for years and was involved with many of the decisions dealing with the local governments. His prominence as a pioneer coupled with his successes in business made him a leading figure in most of the social circles.

Edward Eldridge built a mansion on his homestead overlooking the mouth of Squalicum Creek so Henry built his new home at the other end of his homestead. Perhaps as a show of prominence and wealth to overshadow his old rival, or just to make Elizabeth the happiest woman in the city, Roeder built what may have been the most opulent and finest mansion north of Seattle and maybe even north of San Francisco. Using the finest materials and the best craftsmen, Roeder's new home, which he named "Elmheim", was the one showplace in Whatcom to rival the Fairhaven Hotel at the south end of the bay. The home was finished in 1898 but Elizabeth never lived long enough to witness its completion. Her passing the year before left the home to be occupied only by her grieving husband, daughter Lottie and her husband Charles Roth.

Henry lived in Elmhiem until his death in 1902 but his daughter and her husband continued to reside there.

**The Roeder Mansion "Elmheim" c1910. Jim Doidge collection**

The Roths remodeled the house after Henry's passing and added an addition to the north side of the house. There was a ballroom that occupied most of the third floor along with a secret room that could only be entered by pushing against a fake wall that pivoted on a center pin. Valuables such as jewelry and silverware were kept in this and another secret room that was located on a lower floor.

Lottie and Charles lived in Elmheim until she died in 1933. After her death, Charles moved into the Roth Apartments while the Gages, the in-laws of his son Victor, moved into the mansion.

George Gage and his wife lived in the Roth Mansion for a short time before moving out. The house was subsequently owned by Max and Emma Ebert, J. N. and L. Agnes Akin, Holly and Goldie Simpson, Clyde and Margaret Cory, and Goldie E. Simpson.

In May of 1946 Mrs. Simpson sold the house to Selma and George Merrin. They proceeded to run a bed and breakfast business from that time on.

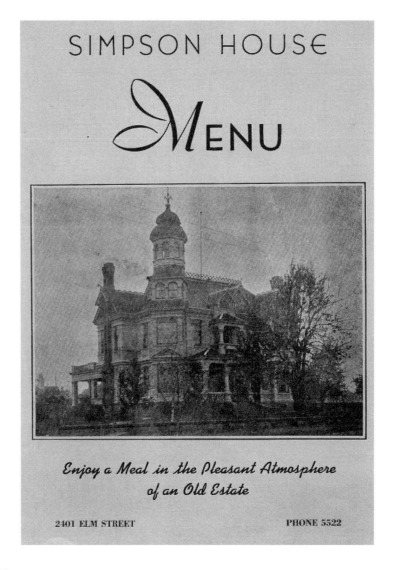

**1946 Simpson House menu**

As time went by, up-keep on the house began to take a financial toll on the owners. Repairs and general up-keep were a drain on the profit margins of the business. Above the upper floor ballroom dwelled a giant honey bee hive. Hundreds of dead bees littered the dance floor and Mrs. Merrin knew that it was only a matter of time before something had to be done and whatever it was wasn't going to be cheap; it was time to sell Elmhiem.

In 1956 Burton Glazer bought the home for $23,000 with the intent of building apartments. The property was ideal but the house did not fit into his plans. It was offered to the Bellingham Historical Society for $7,500 with the intent of moving it to Elizabeth park but neighborhood posturing squelched the plan and it was torn down.

The apartment plan fell through and it took over 21 years before anything was built on the property. It is ironic that the house that was built for Elizabeth was not able to be moved to the park that was named for her. Another irony is the fact that if the transaction had taken place a couple of decades later, the house would probably have been put on the Historical Register and would have been protected from demolition.

**The Roeder Home in 1955. George Krienke photo**

**One of the fireplaces in the Roeder Home. George Krienki photo**

**One of the windows in the mansion. George Krienki photo**

**An interior door. Interior photographs courtesy of George Krienke**

**Elmheim can be seen in the upper left area of this blowup of the photo taken by Sandison in a ballon over Bellingham in 1912. the house sits on the end of the block by itself. It is the largest structure in the area. The trolley is turning onto Broadway from Girard Street.**

**The site of Elmheim in 2008. The lot, originally cleared for the construction of an aparment complex, sat empty for several decades. Eventually, The Elmcrest Apartments were built. By that time, the rest of the block was used for private homes and the City Center Motel, now called the Lions Inn Motel.**

## The Visit of the USS Constitution

Galen Biery papers and photographs #560
Center for Pacific Northwest Studies
Western Washington Unviersity
Bellingham, WA 98225

**On July 14, 1933, the USS Constitution entered Bellingham Bay on her historic voyage to ports of call in the U. S.**

**Greetings… Bellingham Herald**
This 1933 "broadside" depicts the USS Constitution being welcomed by a Bellingham family. Businesses all over the county used photos and sketches of the vessel to promote their products and services. The Navy requested and received assurances that no merchandise would be sold within 3000 feet of the dock.

Howard Buswell papers and photographs #692
Center for Pacific Northwest Studies
Western Washington University
Bellingham, WA 98225

**Boaters greeting the USS Constitution as she docks in Bellingham.**

The USS Constitution was decommissioned in Boston in 1897 where she was rescued from the scrapyard in 1905 by public demand. For a short time she was used as a national museum but in 1925 a complete renovation was initiated with money from numerous organizations and public school drives.

**The USS Constitution sat at dock-side in Bellingham from July 14th to the 20th as she awaited the throngs of local citizens who got a chance to tour the venerable symbol of American independence and power.**
**The belching Puget Sound Pulp and Timber Company's smokestack is a reminder that not long ago, industrial pollution on Bellingham Bay was a very real problem that would take many years of environmental activism to control.**

**Tens of thousands of visitors went aboard the USS Constitution during her visit in Bellingham.**

The USS Constitution was recommissioned on July 1st 1931 with a 21-gun salute. She sailed on a tour of 90 United States ports along the Pacific, Atlantic and Gulf coasts (She was actually towed by the destroyer USS Grebe). Bellingham was the ship's most northerly port of call.

On May 7th 1934, she returned to Boston where she resides to this day as the oldest commissioned ship in the US Navy.

#1 – Sehome Grade School
#2 – Lincoln Grade School
#3 – Franklin Grade School
#4 – Eureka/Roosevelt Grade School

An early view from Sehome Hill shows four schools that no longer exist. All of them except for Eureka were grade schools that served a large population of children who lived in the York neighborhood and surrounding vicinities during the early part of the 20th Century. Franklin, Lincoln and Sehome grade schools have been replaced with Carl Cozier grade school. Eureka/Roosevelt grade school was torn down and a new Roosevelt grade school was built a few blocks away.
Today Laurel Park occupies part of the ground where Sehome Grade School stood. Franklin School is now Franklin Park, Shuksan Healthcare Center sits on the Lincoln School foot print and apartments are found where Eureka School once stood. Whatcom Museum collection

# The Aftermath Club

**The Aftermath Club as it looked in 1908**

The Aftermath Club was formed in 1895 as a lady's reading circle. The members would visit each other and discuss books and other forms of enlightenment and entertainment as befitting the socially conscious group. At one point the group grew large enough that they decided to build a clubhouse. The money was raised (a loan from a members' husband) and a fine building soon sat on the northeast corner of Holly and Broadway. Completed in 1905, the clubhouse had a nicely designed exterior with a fine sandstone chimney. The interior included a reception/meeting room with a kitchen and bathrooms on the main floor, and a ballroom upstairs, with the finest wood trim available.

The club held monthly meetings at which they invited speakers, usually from the college, to tell them about such things as the Greek Isles or the music of the natives of an Asian country or the ancient statues of some Middle Eastern city. Various musicians performed in the clubhouse and plays were presented.

During the wars, the club was the site of groups of women knitting socks for the troops or holding various drives for some sort of community and civic activities.
In 1977, the club sold the building to Jack Westford, a local mortician, but the members continued to meet in the building until 2003, when the club was disbanded.

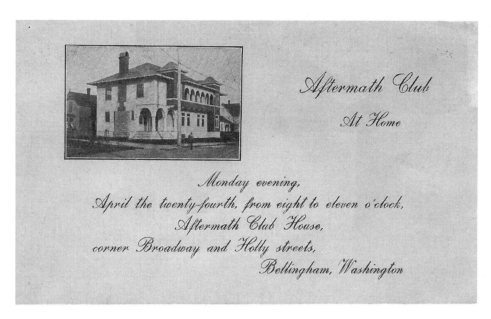

**An invitation to a function in the Aftermath Club in 1940**

Most of the club functions involved some sort of music or guest speaker. Many of the staff at the Normal School lectured at the monthly meetings. Started as a reading circle, the club expanded into various social events and held speaking programs and put on musicals and plays.

**The Aftermath Club building in 2008. The original wood paneling still covers the interior walls of the upper floor. Only the color of the exterior has changed in 103 years.**

The Aftermath Club, now renamed Broadway Hall, is rented out for various functions including civic and private meetings, weddings, and other celebrations. Photos of the interior can be found on the Westford Funeral Home website.

## The Baker Hotel

The largest building in Sehome was the Baker Hotel, built in 1888. In most of the photographs of Sehome taken from 1891 through 1920, the Baker dominated the skyline. Originally built as the Grand Central Hotel, the Baker was the largest hotel north of Seattle.

Galen Biery papers and photographs #1415
Center for Pacific Northwest Studies
Western Washington University
Bellingham, WA 98225

**The Baker Hotel sits on the right edge of the photo in this 1888 panorama of Sehome. The building dominates the town. Note the many stumps and logs left over from the clearing of the lots.**

The Baker was a bad investment from the start. Built by the Carolyn and Jones Real Estate Investment firm of Sehome, the hotel had 140 rooms. Half of them were never opened. In an effort to make money, the hotel was rented to Saint Luke's Hospital for several years until the BBIC donated the land on Ellis and Jersey Streets to build a hospital and nurse's school.

Even new investors couldn't help the business. By 1907, E. B. Deming and a group of investors tried to make a go of keeping the hotel open. By 1913, the hotel wasn't even listed in the city business directory. By the early 1920s, the building was a derelict and finally burned down. In 1927, the Donovan-Flynn auto dealership was built on the site. Later the site was owned by Swan's Moving Company office and warehouse. The building was remodeled and occupied by Community Food Co-Op in the 1980s and has been a popular hang-out for lovers of organic food and good lunches since.

This photo was taken in 1905, shortly after the current owner had spent $50,000 in a major remodeling which also included a new Chuckanut Sandstone lower floor. Forest Street is still just a cleared strip. The street wouldn't be opened for a few more years. Stenton photo

The driver of the hotel stage awaits a call to go pick someone up at the Sehome Dock or one of the train depots in this 1905 photo. The hotel was also served by the trolleys that passed by it going up East Holly Street.

A postcard advertisement for the Hotel Baker in 1907. At this time E. B. Deming and his group owned the hotel. Deming was also a business partner and manager of the Pacific American Fish Company (PAF).

This 2008 photo shows the exterior of the Community Food Co-Op store. Very little change has been made to the exterior since it was built in 1927.

## Tennis at Broadway Park

**This view of East Broadway park around 1912 shows tennis players enjoying an afternoon game of tennis. The courts were built by the city in 1911 in the midst of a tremendous upswing of the local popularity of tennis. Courts were being built in and around Bellingham and tennis clubs were being formed. During this time there were thoughts of supplying every school in town with a court.**
**Galen Biery photo #1621, Center for Pacific NW Studies**

**During the following years, the novelty of the sport began to flatten out. World War I and the coming depression took their toll on the sport's popularity. Basic economic survival trumped casual recreation for many average citizens, leaving the courts open for the few people who were still financially comfortable during those years. By the time the 1950s rolled around, the tennis courts in Broadway Park were long gone, possibly the result of poor drainage. The area where they existed was returned to grass and during the late 50s that portion of the park was flooded by the fire department during winter cold snaps to allow the city's children the chance to ice skate.**

## The Bellingham Federal Office Building

Provincial attitudes brimmed to the surface during the construction of the new Federal Building in Bellingham in May of 1911. Word had gotten out that the federally assigned contractor would be using stone from New Bedford, Indiana instead of the regional darling, Chuckanut sandstone.

**Charles I. Roth**

With construction costs estimated in the $320,000 range, local mover, shaker and Chuckanut quarry owner Charles I. Roth was in hot pursuit of the lucrative stone work that would be required during the building's construction. He held private meetings with J. H. Weise, the contractor, with the expectation of convincing him to change the building specifications to include his Chuckanut quarried stone. Weise was unmoved by the pleas of the local business man and redirected Roth's complaint to the supervising architect, James Knox Taylor.

Taylor (1857-1929) was the supervising architect of the Treasury of The United States from 1897 to 1912 and was responsible for designing many of the larger federal post offices in the country. His buildings are scattered all over the nation and represent some of the finest "classic style-Beaux-arts" structures in the U.S.

Roth was a big fish in Whatcom County and counted the mayor as one of his supporters. His local influence was fairly strong but now he found himself swimming in a much larger pond with Taylor. The fight for local sandstone was a non-starter from the beginning because the government set contracts that best suited its interests; it was a forgone conclusion that the contract for Indiana stone was not negotiable at the local level.

J.P.DeMattos, the mayor of Bellingham was furious over the failure of the local stone contracting and let it be known when he attempted an unsuccessful veto of a city council vote to allow for Magnolia and Dock streets to be partially blocked during the Federal Building's construction. In a dissenting comment directed at the outside parties involved in the request for exemption from existing city street ordinances, he stated the following:

"If you think a premium should be granted for such independence by a foreign contractor vote "aye" pass the ordinance over this veto and give newcomers to understand that home loyalty and civic pride are a negligible quantity in Bellingham."

The mayor's veto statement was answered by councilman Sells with the following comment:

"Perhaps the contractor and the supervising architect in Washington D.C. knew what they were talking about when they specified Indiana stone. I have heard that, like some person's head, Chuckanut stone is soft. That may be the reason the contract was given for Indiana stone."

In the end, the contractor was allowed to use part of the streets for material staging and work began in earnest to get the plot ready for construction.

On September 11th 1911 the corner stone was put into position at the corner of Dock and Magnolia. The laying of the corner stone was under the direction of the Masons and led by State Grand Mason D.S. Prescott. In a special compartment under the stone, the pictures of Congressman William E. Humphrey and J.H Bloedel along with a copy of the latest Bellingham Herald Sunday paper were sealed. Hundreds of people including a large contingent of Masons witnessed the ceremony as the York band played rousing patriotic music.

Near the end of April 1913, the Federal Building was completed and several Federal agencies including the post office, department of immigration and department of commerce and labor began to move in.

**A view of the Federal Building during construction. The construction office sits out in Magnolia Street. The first telephone exchange building sits to the right.**

A photo of the building during the beginning of construction can be found on the table of contents page. The removal of the sandstone for the basement delayed the construction and cost in excess of $20,000.

In the 21st century, the Federal Building is still a magnificent and functioning structure. After 95 years the Indiana stone has proven to be a wise choice and the perceived indignity of "trampled local pride" seems to have been buried deep within the bedrock below.

In this 1932 photo taken by Jacobson, the Federal Building sits in the center of downtown Bellingham, surrounded by the major commercial establishments. The Montague and McHugh Department Store is on the corner of Commercial and Magnolia. The Cissna Apartments are in the left distance. The Douglas Block sits behind the Montague and McHugh block. The tower on the Bellingham Hotel pokes up over the roof of the Federal Building. Jacobson photo

The Federal Building in 2008. The Bon Marche is now the Crown Plaza Building. the tower on the Bellingham Hotel was damaged in a storm in the mid-1930s and removed.

## TERRIFIC RACE WON BY EVERETT SPEED FIEND

*Traveling for all the world like a rocket, leaving behind her a trail of smoke and fire, her exhausts pounding like a miniature battery of field artillery, Highball, the little twenty foot hyhdroplane owned by Bailey Hilton, of Everett, won the first heat of the twenty foot Puget Sound championship races at Lake Whatcom this morning, with Nahua I, the property of the Kent-Marvin company, a good second.*

*The Nahua I made the last two rounds with a big hole in her bottom. Heading close inshore on the last round, her driver, Carl Folsom, drove her nose across the finish line in front of the grandstand just as the speedboat disappeared under the water. Folsom, swathed in lifebelts, leaped as his craft went down, and splashed ashore. Nothing like the race was ever seen on Lake Whatcom before, and but for the fact that several of the competitors were forced to retire owing to machine trouble of one sort or another, there is no question but that a new record for the Pacific Coast would have been chalked up if not new figures for twenty foot boats of the world. Thousands upon thousands of visitors lined the shores of the lake and filled the grandstand of the Lake Whatcom Motorboat club, packing the steamship and transportation vessels plying on the lake to capacity. The wind, which arose blustering and threatening in the morning, had died away to a fairly stiff breeze, not strong enough to in any way endanger the various racing craft, but yet sufficient to apply to the pilots and engineers a supreme test of skill.*

*Four boats in all entered the twenty foot race-the Potlatch Bug, owned by the Schertzer Brothers, of Seattle, and equipped with a great 100 horsepower Emerson engine geared up to 2 to1 on the propeller; the Highball, owned by Bailey Hilton, of Everett, and equipped with a lttle twenty-four horsepower Fairbanks Morse racing engine; the Nahua I, owned by the Kent-Marvin company, of Bellingham, and equipped with a big forty horsepower standard Roberts engine and driven by Carl Folsom, and the Br'er Fox, of Olympia, equipped with a great fifty horsepower Fox deluxe engine and driven be H. H. Manny.*

*The boats got away to a splendid start, the Potlatch Bug, racing like a mad thing, being first to cross the line, the Nahua I and the Highball at her heels. Then plunging and nosing the choppy water comes the Br'er Fox. This is the first time the boat has been in the water and her engine is set too far forward, but it is too late to make any change.*

*Slowly but surely the great power of the Potlatch Bug begins to make itself felt. Running easily, the little Seattle boat draws slowly to the front, the Nahua and the Highball racing side by side in as pretty a contest as ever took place on Lake Whatcom roany other place close behind her. The Br'er Fox is already trailing steadily behind.*

*And so they run for the first two laps, the Highball gaining a little upon the Nahua and the Potlatch Bug drawing further-even further- in the lead. At the close of the second round it is plain that, barring accidents, the race is to go to the Bug, with the Highball and Nahua I fighting neck and neck for second place. But the Providence that reserves special dipensations for the motorboat racer had other things in view.*

*The Potlatch Bug broke down. For five minutes Frank Schertzer and Stanley Miller get busy with the machinery. The Nahua and the Highball sweep past her like a torrent. Then with the other two boats well nigh a full lap in the lead the Bug starts with a snort. Down the lake she comes in the most terrific effort, perhaps, ever seen on water. The little boat leaps, time after time, clear of the lake like something living, her exhaust humming like a swarm of giant bees and the spectators fairly gasp as she tries to make up the interval. Now she hits a swell, and for an instant the entire boat is lost in a cataract of spray, now she rounds a buoy and a great rainbow is thrown by her rudder, but all the time the interval between her and the Nahua, now third in the race, is steadily growing smaller by degrees and beautifully less.*

*Rearing on her end like a blooded horse pawing the air, snorting and roaring, she sweeps past the grandstand at fifty miles an hour, and the air is rent with the roar of excited spectators. Again she completes the lap, passing from sight in a flash and just below the clubhouse, almost in the act of taking second place, her machinery gives out a second time.*

*One can almost feel the pity of the multitude for the gallant little Seattle racer, but it is just such things as those that are meant to be tested in the long twenty mile grind.*

*Never varying a foot in her place, plugging steadily ahead, the Highball is now well in the lead, with the Na-*

*hua, a great hole in her bottom from hitting some sort of a snag, pounding and laboring behind with a dogged courage and perseverance that brought round after round of applause. Carl Folsom swathed in lifebelts and begoggled like a diver, getting out of his boat every ounce of speed in her. Far in the rear trails the Br'er Fox, accepting the fortune of war with a splendid grace and ready to start again tomorrow.*

*This is the order until the end. A rousing cheer greated Higball as she crossed the line and another for the Nahua. To say that enthusiasm marked the progress of the race would be to put it mildly. It is unlikely, indeed, that anything like the excitement prevailing during the attempt of the Potlatch Bug to get back into the race ever before characterized a contest on the Pacific Coast.*

*The speed of the Highball is considered terrific for this class of boat. By covering the full course of twenty miles in 43½ minutes the little craft made an average speed of 27.58 miles an hour.*

Bellingham Herald, July 23, 1912.

**The smoke was thick and the noise deafening as these racers took off from Silver Beach in 1912. The Lake Whatcom Motor Club had been formed three years earlier when some well to-do local racing enthusiasts decided to have organized competitions on the lake. Races like this were held for several years and brought competitors from all over the Sound. The organization built a clubhouse at Watkins point to conduct their meetings and have social gatherings. By 1916 the group disbanded when the novelty and interest in racing lost steam. Charles Cissna took over the building and it continued as a rental hall until it burned in 1919. Sandison photo Whatcom Museum collection**

# The Two Routes of I-5

To most people who drive through Bellingham on Interstate 5, the thought of having to navigate Samish Way, Ellis St., Holly St., Prospect St. and Northwest Ave. just to get through town would seem absurd today. Passing above Happy Valley, through the York and Sunnyland neighborhoods and out around the Country Club has been a familiar and convenient route for travelers for years. Few people realize that there was a time when a different route through Bellingham was considered and was actually favored by the city.

When Dwight Eisenhower became president, he set about getting legislation passed to create an Interstate highway system. It would be modeled somewhat on the German Autobahn system that he saw in Europe at the end of World War ll. His administration saw the need to develop a series of limited access highways that could be used for the quick deployment of men and weapons to anywhere in the United States and for the quick evacuation of people from cities in case of nuclear war.

The prospect of a conflict with the U.S.S.R. seemed like a real possibility during the 50s and most citizens saw that assumption as a fact of life. Most people from the baby boom generation remember the school evacuation drills of the 50s and 60s.

It was noted that rolling commerce could operated more efficiently than it had been to that point. Goods and services could be transported faster and cheaper if trucks could avoid the painstakingly slow traversing of city streets. Keeping the trucks in higher gears for longer durations saved fuel, money and the time it took to get products to the market place. This, in turn, would help lower the costs of goods for the consumer.

The debate in Bellingham centered on the advantages of building the freeway along the waterfront as opposed to building it further inland and through the neighborhoods east of the central business district. Community leaders where in favor of the waterfront route because they felt that freight should be delivered directly to the business centers that clustered around the waterfront area but the federal government had a different view. They envisioned freeways moving goods and services from Mexico to the Canadian border using the most direct routes possible. Cities like Bellingham, who were losing their manufacturing base, held little sway with the Government when it came to route selection and the budgeting of Federal funds also played a significant roll. The waterfront route would have cost in excess of $15 million to construct "think Alaska Way Viaduct". The cost of the inland route was estimated at a considerably smaller sum of around $6 million.

The waterfront route would have begun at 34th St. and the Old Samish road and headed west. Swinging north, it would have crossed Kellogg St. at about 25th St. between Connelly and Lindsay Ave. Its westerly route would have taken it under the 12th St. Bridge and right in front of Fairhaven Middle School. It would have swung north and created a major cloverleaf and underpass at Harris Ave. at 10th St.

It would have then followed the Boulevard/S. State St. route until it got to Oak St. then a long bridging structure would have passed over the rail tracks and Railroad Ave. to Laurel St. just east of Cornwall Ave. The freeway would have gone under Cornwall, Chestnut St. and Bay St. Another long structure would then have been built from I St. to Williams St. to pass over the railroad tracks again as the highway went out Roeder Ave. The major interchange would have been at Central Ave.

A lengthy structure would have been built to carry the freeway up over the railroad spurs to the Squalicum Creek industrial area and the highway would then have passed under Eldridge Ave. at about Madrona St.
 There would have been a bridge over Squalicum Creek and an underpass and exchange at Nequalicum Ave. and another bridge at Little Squalicum Creek near the cement plant. An overpass would have been needed for the cement plant rail spur and an underpass for Bennett Ave. just north of the Marietta road.
 The freeway would then have headed north as it paralled Bennett with a crossing at Alderwood Ave. to its

intersection with the completed freeway north of Bakerview Rd.

Much to the chagrin of the city business leaders, the state opted for the inland or "Lincoln Street route namely because of the vast difference in cost of construction.

The plan called for the freeway to run between Samish Way and 32nd St. and then turn north along Lincoln St. and over Meador Ave. It would continue along Lincoln St. go over Iowa St. and under Alabama St. and then cut its way just east of Memorial Park. It would continue north under Sunset Drive before turning northwest. Running just south of the Moonlight Drive-In it would pass by the Country Club, over Northwest Ave. and under Bakerview Rd.

The route required the purchase of land through the heart of the city. It would cause the displacement of many family homes and the physical alterations of some of the older neighborhoods.

The York neighborhood was gutted through the middle. Neighbors found themselves separated from each other by four lanes of traffic and a chain link fence. Children lost playmates that'd moved away with their parents after their homes were bought by the state.

The division continued up through the Sunnyland neighborhood where part of Memorial Park was claimed by the state with a deep clay cut taking part of the east edge of the main property and a third of the park being cut away north of Illinois St. A pedestrian bridge was installed so the children on the east side of the freeway could still attend grade school with their friends.

Similar examples of dissection occurred all along the route but in the end, the freeway's construction ultimately resulted in the ability to quickly and easily traverse the city.

It has been almost fifty years since the city neighborhoods where split and the wounds have pretty much scared over. Many of the people who live in the neighborhoods now don't remember the time before the freeway changed the landscape. Most people under fifty years of age see the freeway as a familiar part of the terrain but for others, the wounds have taken a little longer to heal.

The brighter side of the decision to build the inland route would be the fact that a coastal route would have destroyed Fairhaven and isolated the waterfront from the community. The people of Bellingham and their relationship to the waterfront would have suffered a virtual disconnect that in all likelihood would have never been mended.

**Contractors discussing the Alabama Street overpass during the construction of the Interstate through Bellingham. Whatcom Museum collection**

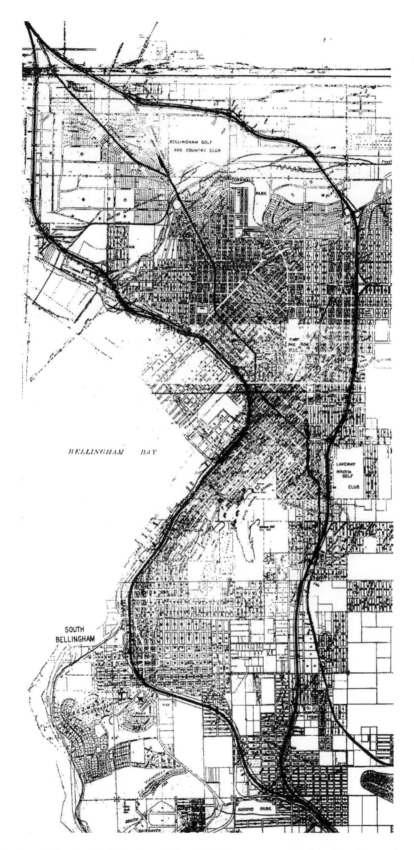

**This map was displayed in the Bellingham Herald Newspaper during the discussion on where the freeway should go. Both routes are shown, as well as the Highway 99 route which is represented by a thinner line.**

# Going ashore, the docks on the bay

The Sehome dock around 1905. Peter Hegg's photo captured the "Californian" tied up at the dock.

The Sehome dock in 1910. The original dock was built in the mid 1850s and serviced the community and coal mine. In this photo, the dock business depicts the major transportation of the period. "Mosquito Fleet" boats bringing passengers and freight to Bellingham from the other cities on the sound while railroad box cars wait to be loaded or unloaded. Trolleys wait for the passengers get off the boats.

The Ocean dock in Fairhaven. This dock was next to the one built by Dan Harris. The ship is delivering timbers and rail for the construction of the Fairhaven and Southern railway which would go from Fairhaven to Sedro Woolley and the Cokedale coal mine. The delivery of the rails was delayed for about six months due to the original order being destroyed in the Great Seattle Fire in 1889. The Colony dock site is now the site of the Bellingham Ferry Terminal.

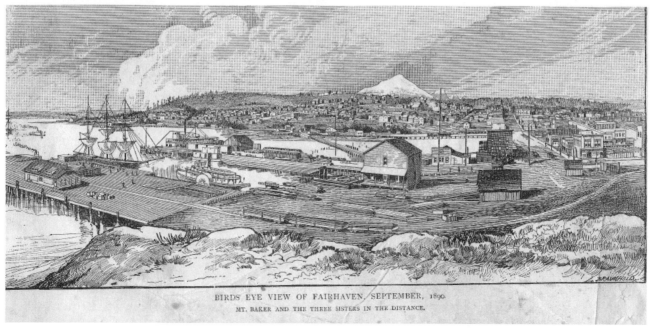

An artists drawing of Fairhaven in the magazine "The Fairhaven" in 1890 shows the docks. Dan Harris' hotel is at the foot of McKenzie Avenue. The Fairhaven magazine was sent to the eastern cities as a promotional item.

Galen Biery papers and photographs #1598
Center for Pacific Northwest Studies
Western Washington University
Bellingham, WA 98225

**Another photo of the docks at Fairhaven, taken during the construction of the railroad through Fairhaven and north along the bay past Whatcom in 1890. The railroad trestle across the mouth of Padden Creek is already complete.**

**In 1891, the bay in front of New Whatcom was being filled by the GN railroad trestle and the C Street and Colony Docks. The docks were built out into deeper water so that ships didn't have to unload cargo onto barges. The Railroad crossed the bay so that the shoreline could be developed for industry. It was still a long trip for passengers to get to the depots. A swing bridge in the railroad trestle allowed smaller boats and barges to get closer to shore. The Globe Mill is just being completed. The BBIC Mill is out of the photo on the left. Whatcom Museum collection**

The steamer Kulshan at the new Citizens Dock in 1913. The Kulshan was built in 1912 and was a regular visitor to Bellingham. The waterway was dredged every few years so that ships could get to the dock. The dredgings were deposited in lagoons along the shore to make dry land on the tide flats. Hall photo

The Princess Sophia at Citizens Dock in 1915. The Sophia was one of the Canadian Pacific Railroad Company boats that sailed along the west coast from Alaska to Bellingham. On October 23, 1918, the ship left Juneau, Alaska and ran onto the rocks at Vanderbilt Reef. All 353 passengers and crew were lost. Banks photo

In this photo taken from a balloon in 1912 by Sandison, the Whatcom Creek Waterway is on the right, the Morrison Mill is in the center, and the BBIC Mill is along the left shoreline. The Sehome and BBIC docks are in the distance. The dredgings from the waterway are being used to fill in the tide flats between the Morrison Mill and Chestnut Street. The view is looking south from above Commercial and Grand Streets. Whatcom Museum photo

The Sehome dock about 1960. The frame structure is on the railroad dock, where rail cars were loaded onto barges for the trip to other ports on Puget Sound. The ship is tied up at the south end of the Port of Bellingham Dock.

In the early 1980s, the Citizens Dock was considered for rehabilitation as a historical site, museum, waterfront shops, and a number of other useful purposes. By the time the city quit dragging their feet, the dock had deteriorated to the point that it was beyond repair. In 1987, it was torn down and the piling removed.

The remains of the Sehome Dock and the rail car loading dock in 2008. Photo taken from the foot of Cornwall Avenue next to the Port of Bellingham Terminal.

A land without ruins is a land without memories --- and a land without memories is a land without history.     Abram Joseph Ryan

## Once you've seen the elephants...

From almost the beginning of Bellingham's existence, traveling shows seemed to have found their way to the bay. Countless performers of all kinds including minstrels in wagons, small vaudeville acts, magicians and jugglers plied their trade for anyone who would give them the time of day and a few dollars in the pot.

During the early years, the towns that clustered on Bellingham Bay were still very much in the backwater when compared against much of America. Few roads were planked much less paved so when given the chance, people would flock to see someone from the outside world perform an act or sing a song.

Before the railroads were built, the shows came first by ship and later by wagon. The mode of transportation limited the size of the shows to a few dozen performers. The big shows would come with the arrival of the railroad in the early 1890s and one of the biggest arrived on August 17th 1903.

The 85 cars of the Ringling Brothers Circus rolled into Whatcom during the early hours of August 17th after leaving Spokane the previous day. The popularity of circuses during the early part of the 20th Century was due, in part, to the fact that there was little competition in the form of other diversions. Movies were in their absolute infancy, practical radio was years away and television only dwelled in the minds of inventors and science fiction writers; entertainment options were bleak.

A Whatcom Reveille reporter was sent to attend the circus and write a column for the next day's paper, this is what he said:

*A wonderful show - the largest and most wonderful circus in the world; a vast throng of people – the largest crowd that has ever been seen in Whatcom. This expresses briefly the main points connected with the visit here yesterday of Ringling Brothers Circus. It is estimated that nearly 20,000 people gathered beneath the great stretch of canvas to watch the afternoon performance; while an almost equal number attended the evening show. This is certainly the largest crowd that ever attended a circus in Whatcom. It was unofficially stated that $26.000 was taken in at the gate here yesterday. Every train and boat from the various outlying districts and surrounding towns in this and adjacent counties was loaded down with those who had come to see the one thing that can draw all the people all of the time – Ringling's great show. Hundreds of others came in with wagons and carriages, and nearly everyone on the Bay attended one or the other of the performances. There were men, women and children of every type and description, all actuated by the same general motive.*

*The show arrived here early in the morning, and by 12 o'clock everything had been put in shape, and the grand street parade was given. The streets along which the parade was passing were literally jammed with sight-seers. The parade, it may be stated, was probably the best the Ringling Brothers have ever given here. Great troops of camels and elephants were the special attraction; while the steam calliope, perfectly played, gave the parade a strictly "circus" effect.*

*By two o'clock the great tents on the B.B.I. Company's field were rapidly filling with the throng. The side shows did a good business; everybody wanted to see the three-legged boy, the two headed man, the dwarf, the giant, the snake charmer and the fat lady, and all were satisfied with what they saw. On the grounds there was not the slightest trace of crooks, tinhorns or shell operators; the legitimate and time-honored red lemonade and peanut and popcorn man reigned supreme, and everything was clean and straight.*

*Within the main tent, if the audience exceeded all previous Whatcom audiences, so did the performance surpass, in magnificence and in ability to please all performances of this great circus. The new spectacular feature – "Jerusalem and the Crusades"—was a particularly brilliant effect. The gorgeous costumes of the knights and priests of the various nations were shown in proper style. Peter the Hermit was shown exerting the people to engage in the crusades and the various great leaders of that strenuous time were depicted with apparent accuracy of detail. The work of the oriental dancing girls in this act was a very graceful exhibition, which the pretty costumes of the dancers helped to make more beautiful. Over 500 people and many horses were engaged in this one act.*

*The trained elephants and seals, in their acrobatic and equilibristic feats were a surprise to those who had not closely noted them at previous performances.*

*The trapeze work, done at a dizzy height, commanded the admiration and inspired the awe of the onlookers The man who performed above the center ring almost at the top of the high tent, had a couple of feats which, would seem, should hardly be performed without a net protection in case of a fall.*

*The usual quota of clowns were on deck with all the old chestnut stunts that have been used for centuries in circus work – and a few new ones which were certainly refreshing in comparison with the others.*

*The performances closed with some fast, hair-raising races of all kinds, including, among others, dog races, horse races with monkey jockeys, Roman hippodromes, and the old and thrilling chariot races.*

*The menagerie was better stocked than ever. There was every live thing imaginable, from the huge, loose jointed elephant, the roaring lion, the thick skinned rhinoceros, the monstrous buffalo, to the tender fawn, the guinea-pig and the gaudy cockatoos, and others too numerous to mention.*

*One, who "took in" the whole show, including the concert, could not help but feel that he or she had not seen and heard nearly every possible form of proper entertainment.*

*Immediately after the night performance the work of tearing down the temporary home of the big show and transporting the tents, seats and animals to the cars was begun, and shortly after midnight the start had been made for Everett, where the circus will show today.*

The Reveille  August 18th 1903


The enthusiasm of the reporter mirrored much of the populous at that time; the circus was probably the entertainment highlight of the year for most people. The fact that the circus was able to break down everything, load the cars and move to another city in one night is testament to the tremendous logistical skills developed through years of trial and error. During World War I, the U.S. Army went to Ringling and other circuses to learn the art of loading military trains efficiently. They turned to the circuses for one reason only, they were better at loading personnel and equipment into trains and they could do it faster than anyone else in the world.

Full page advertisement in the Bellingham Reveille, 1903

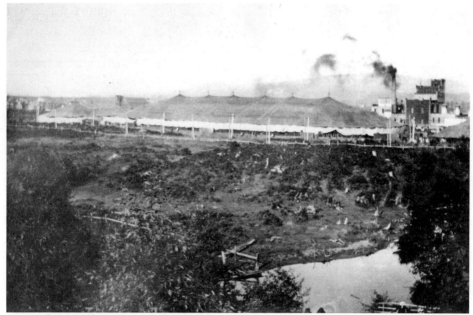

Howard Buswell papers and photographs #535
Center for Pacific Northwest Studies
Western Washington University
Bellingham, WA 98225

**This photograph shows the Ringling Brothers circus tents erected on the Bellingham Bay Improvement field east of Dock Street. The tents stretch from just south of what would become Ohio Street all the way north to Kentucky Street. The field would later be called the Brewery Fair grounds and Dock Street would be changed to Cornwall Avenue. The 3 B Brewery with smoke stack can be seen to the right. The fair grounds would eventually be replaced with Bellingham High School.**

**The same view taken in 2008 looking east. The photo was taken from the upper floor of the former Cascade building. The view is across Whatcom Creek and over the roof of the old Albertson's Market, now the DeWaard and Bode Appliances store. Ohio Street is on the left.**

The circuses put Bellingham Bay on their stops from 1901 through 1908. The Ringling Brothers came to the Brewery grounds every other year. Barnum and Bailey came in 1908.

The seven Ringling brothers started their circus in 1884. Their popularity allowed them to grow, and by 1889, the circus had expanded so much that a special train was needed to haul the circus across country.

In 1882, P. T. Barnum and his travelling show "P. T. Barnum's Great Travelling Museum" merged with the Baily Circus. The result was called the "Greatest Show on Earth". When Barnum died in 1891, James Baily took over the show. When Baily died in 1906, the circus was bought by the Ringling brothers. The shows were separate until 1919, when the circus became the Ringling Brothers and Barnum and Baily Circus. By 1930, the Ringling Brothers had the largest circus in the world. During WWII, the circus was the only thing that travelled by train besides passengers and war materials. In 1944, the main tent caught fire and over 100 people died. Eventually, the popularity of the circus dwindled and the last performance under the big top was on July 16, 1956. The circus was bought in 1967 by a group of investors, and the show was upgraded to a blue and a red section, each with over 100 railroad cars, and a smaller gold section that could accommodate smaller towns and cities. Emphasis is now placed on working with various animal care groups to insure that the elephants and the other working animals receive the best care, although PETA and some other groups still make claims of cruelty due to captivity.

A Herald ad from the 1907 visit of the Ringling Brothers Circus.

**Circus day 1905. The matched team of white horses pulls a calliope up Holly Street.**

The Barnum and Bailey Circus came to town in 1908. The elephants are coming up Holly past the new construction of the Alaska Block on the corner of State and Holly Streets. One of the young people watching the parade was George Loggie's daughter Helen, who went home and drew pictures of the elephants. Helen Loggie later became a world famous artist, scetching most of her scenes around Whatcom County. Whatcom Museum collection

# Maps

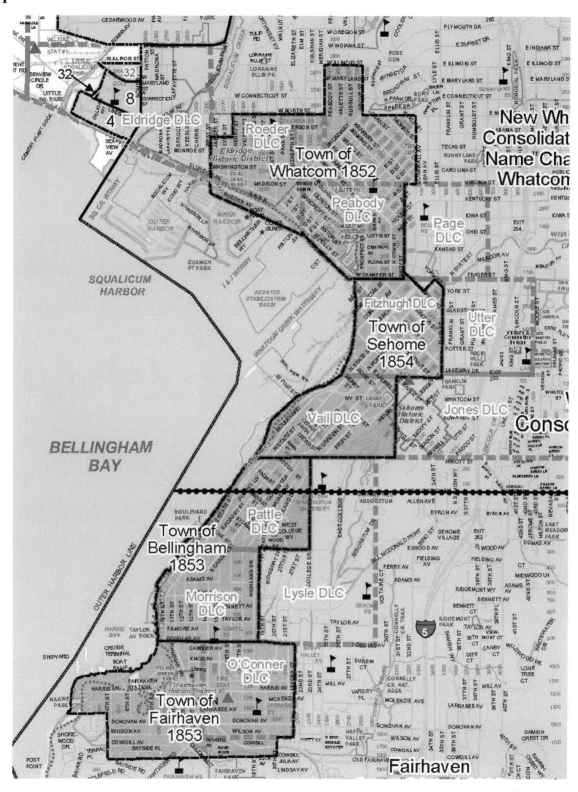

This map shows the layout of the first Donation Land Claims (DLC) and the earliest plats. The dates under the town names represent the earliest known settlement by Europeans. Detail of a map from the City of Bellingham Website.

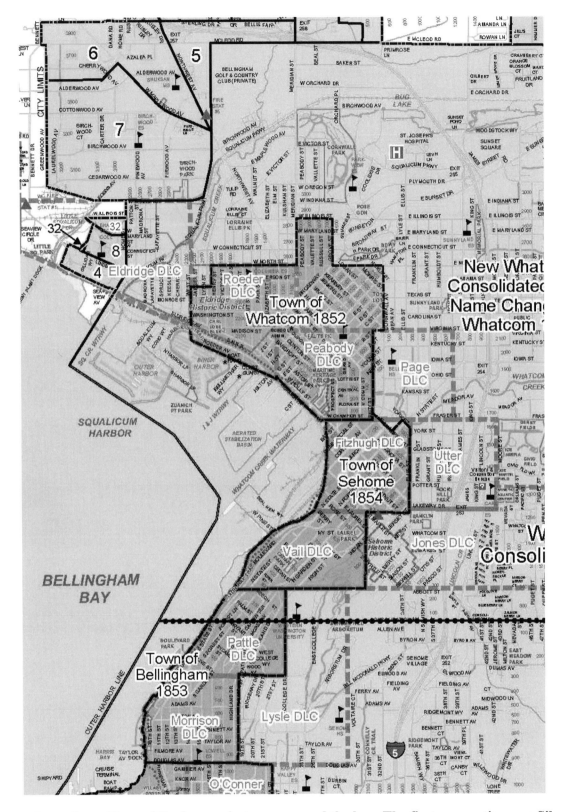

This map shows the outlines of the four main towns around the bay. The first annexation was Silver Beach in 1908, followed by the area from Bloedel Park south to Kansas Street. The third annexation was the strip west from Squalicum Creek to the present-day cement plant area. In all, there have been 34 major annexations. Map from the City of Bellingham Website.

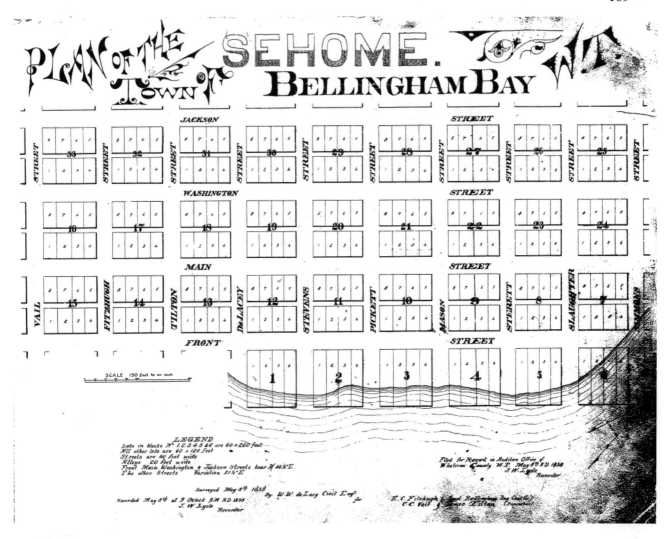

William W. DeLacy's survey of Sehome filed on May 8, 1858 by E. C. Fitzhugh and C. C. Vail

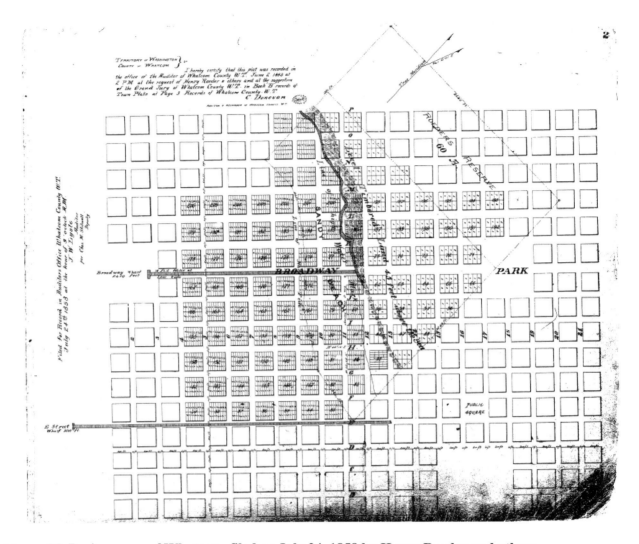

Alonzo M. Poe's survey of Whatcom, filed on July 24, 1858 by Henry Roeder and others.

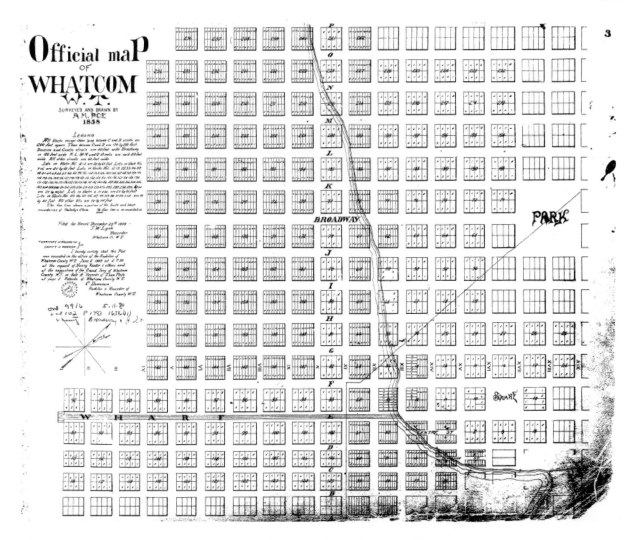

Another filing of Poe's survey of Whatcom, filed on December 25, 1858

Survey of the plat of Bellingham, filed in Seattle on May 10, 1871 for Arthur A. Denny, David Phillips, and Dexter Horton. These men were co-founders of the city of Seattle and Horton owned a bank. These investors included Edward Eldridge. It was rumored that the railroad was going to terminate at Bellingham Bay. War in Europe ended any hope of enough money to bring the railroad north. Hand written notations on the plat map indicate changes made to items such as street changes or name changes. The word vacate or vacation means that the plat or a street was cancelled.

Daniel J. Harris' survey of Fairhaven, filed on January 2, 1883. As noted on the map, the plat was partially vacated on April 9, 1889 after the Fairhaven Improvement Company filed a re-plat.

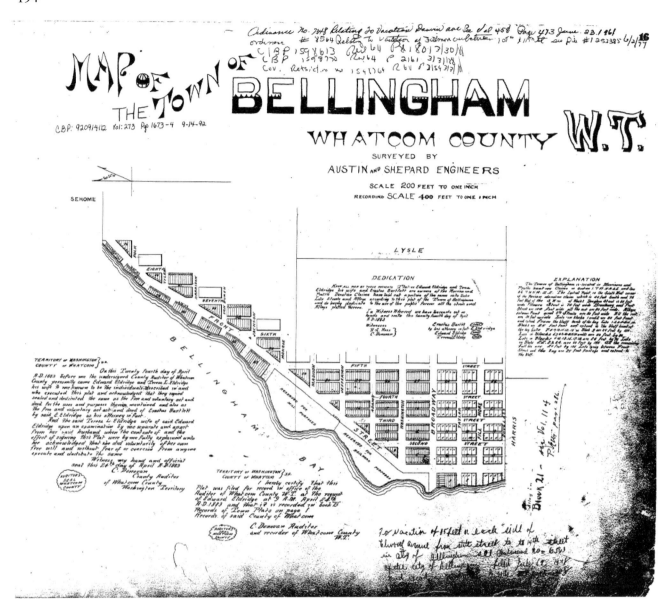

On April 4, 1883, Edward Eldridge and Erastus Bartlett filed a re-plat of the town of Bellingham, possibly due to the Seattle investors pulling out of the partnership. Lack of a railroad and low lot sale numbers most likely were the reason. Eldridge and Bartlett would also be partners in the Red Mill, a saw mill along present-day Boulevard Park and the later site of the E. K. Wood Mill.

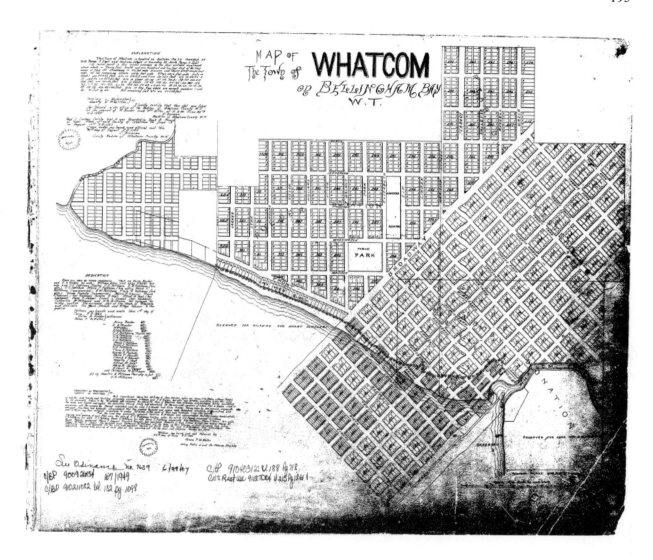

On June 26, 1883, Henry Roeder and C. J. Pettibone, trustee for the Peabody estate, filed a new plat of Whatcom.

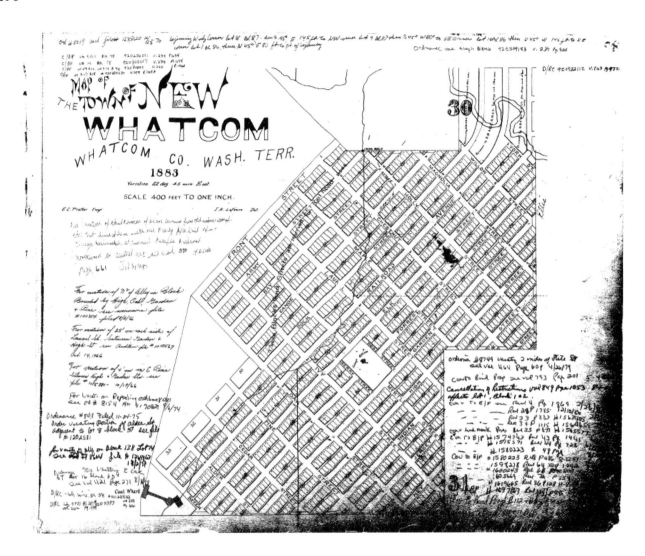

In 1883, E. C. Prather, engineer for the B. B. I. C., filed a plat of New Whatcom. This was the vacant land that had been undeveloped between the towns of Whatcom and Sehome. Sehome was also changed to New Whatcom. Evidently the name change was made to generate an influx of residents and more property sales.

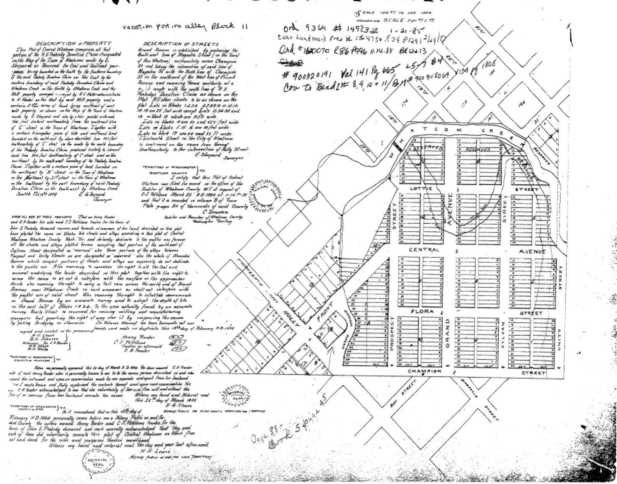

On March 26, 1884, J. C. Pettibone, acting on behalf of the Peabody heirs, filed a plat of the central portion of the city of Whatcom. This was on the east half of the Peabody Donation claim. The meander reserve had been filed on by Roeder earlier. As noted, the streets did not line up. The old original Pickett Bridge is the dark line across the creek. Eventually, all of the streets were re-aligned to match up. An iron bolt had been driven at the center of the intersection of Champion and 13th Streets. The bolt was the marker that separated New Whatcom from Whatcom. The bolt may still be there. Several feet of fill covered the bolt when the street was leveled around 1889.

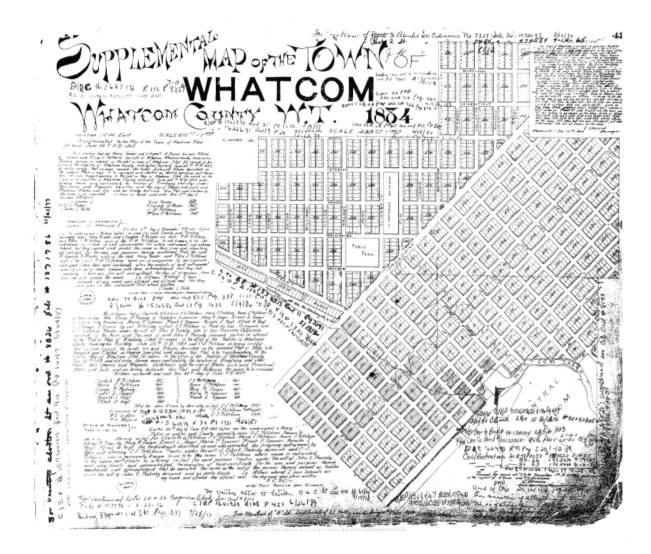

This supplemental plat of Whatcom was filed on November 13, 1885. Adjustments had been made to re-align several streets including Broadway, and the lot sizes were also slightly adjusted.

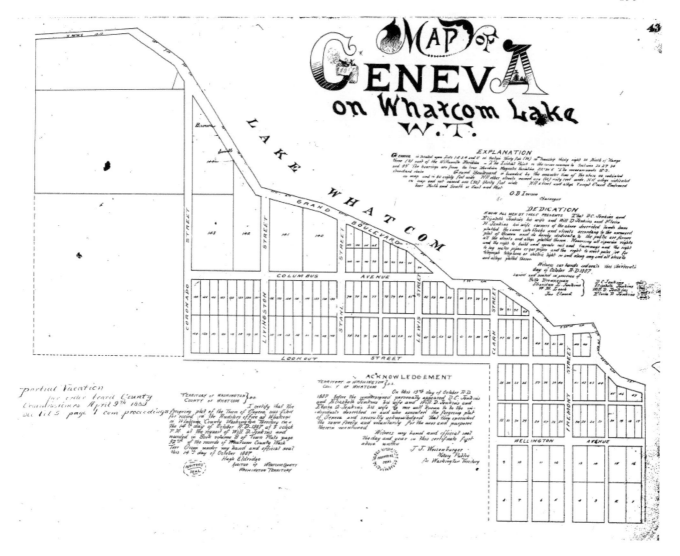

The plat of Geneva was filed on October 13, 1887. Geneva was surveyed by O. B. Iverson for D. C. Jenkins and his wife Elizabeth, and Will Jenkins and his wife Elvira.
Even though Geneva has been along the eastern Bellingham city limits for many years, it still sits outside the city.

The York addition to New Whatcom was filed on July 7, 1888 by Carmin Dibble. The York addition was the first major addition to the city.

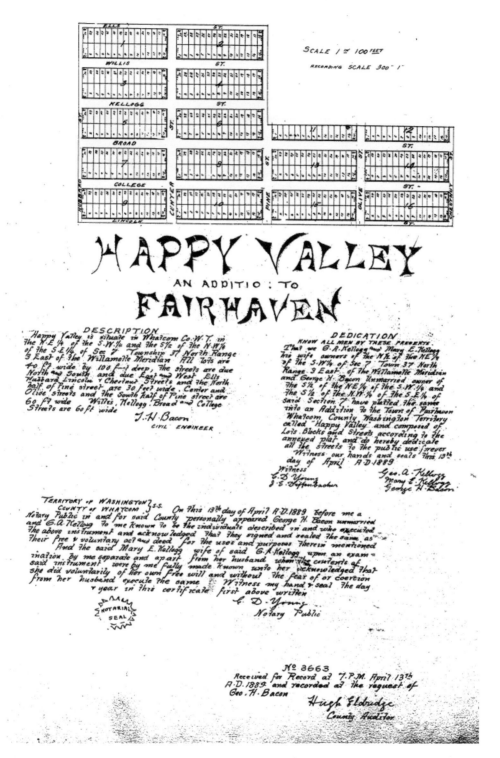

On April 13, 1889, the Happy Valley plat was filed as an addition to Fairhaven by George Bacon and G. A. Kellogg.

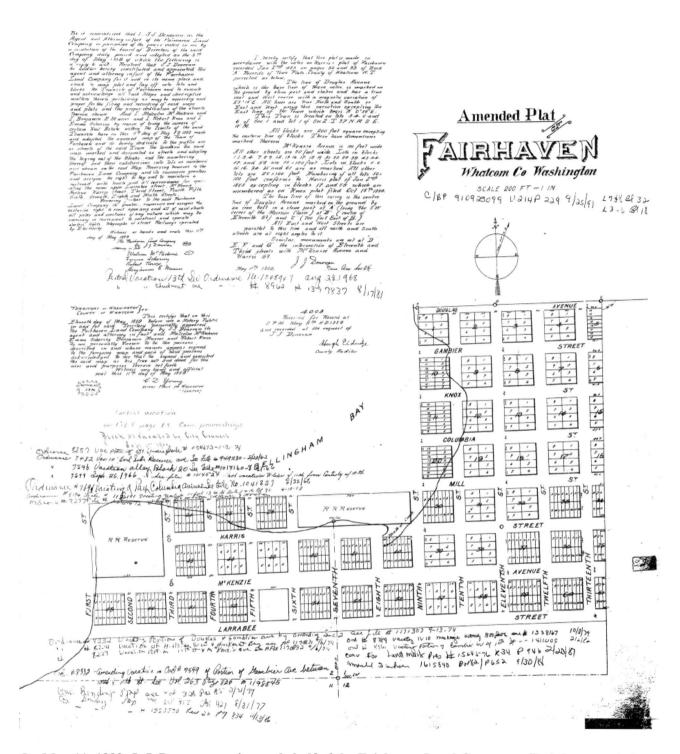

On May 11, 1889, J. J. Donovan, acting on behalf of the Fairhaven Land Company, filed the amended plat of Fairhaven. The plat was filed after the land company, under control of Nelson Bennett and the Fairhaven Improvement Company, bought the townsite from Dan Harris. The Fairhaven Land Company also purchased the old Bellingham townsite from Eldridge and Bartlett. Fairhaven was to be the terminus for the Great Northern Railroad.

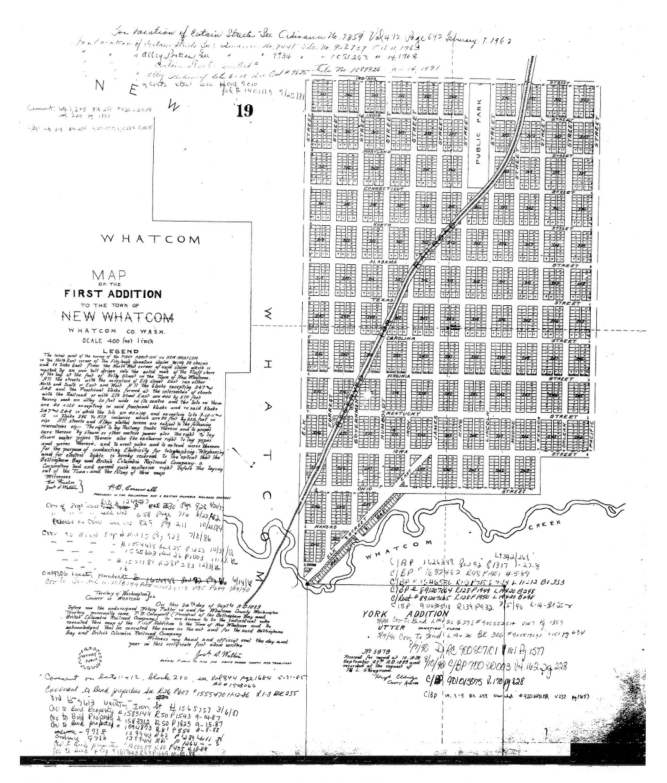

This plat encompasses the property north of the York addition and east of the northern part of the Whatcom city limits. Pierre Cornwall filed the plat on behalf of the Bellingham Bay Improvement Company. Cornwall had bought thousands of acres of property around the bay when he controlled the Sehome Coal Mine. Cornwall was a very astute businessman and knew the value of land. Cornwall also owned the BB&BC railway, which had a right-of-way through the plat.

The Alabama Street addition was filed on March 14, 1890. Pierre Cornwall also owned this property and filed the plat on behalf of the Bellingham Bay and British Columbia Railroad.

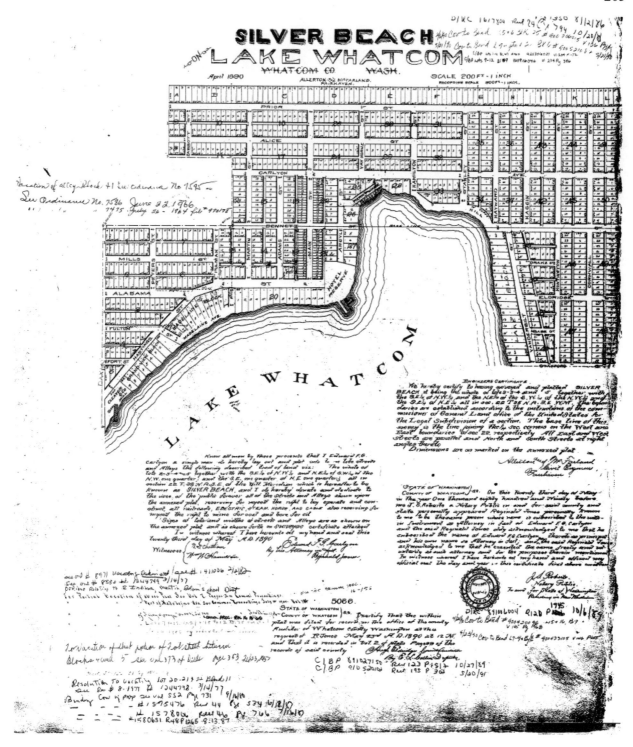

Reginald Jones and Edward F. G. Carlyon filed the plat of Silver Beach on May 23, 1890. Jones and Carlyon were real estate investors who also had several other plats around the Whatcom and New Whatcom townsites. They also owned the huge Grand Central Hotel in New Whatcom. In 1891, they would open the Silver Beach Hotel on the point of land marked for a hotel reserve.

On June 5, 1891, Richard Fenton filed this plat of the Eureka Addition to New Whatcom.

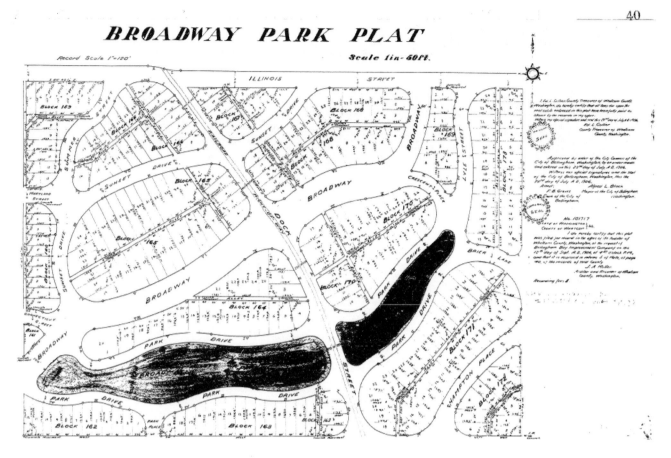

The BBIC filed this plat of the Broadway Park area on July 23, 1906.

On April 2, 1908, the BBIC filed the plat of the Sunnyland neighborhood.

**Front Cover photo, 2008**

It has been nearly 100 years since the ladies posed on the log at this spot. Two world wars and countless other conflicts have visited their pox upon us since that time but the lake still glimmers. Depressions, booms and countless personal stories of triumph and tragedy have played out over the decades but the lake is still nurturing our community every day. With some nurturing of our own, it will continue to provide for us long into the future.

**Back Cover photo**
A representative grouping of old photos is surrounded by a outline of the 2008 Bellingham City Limits. The current city is several times larger than it was when it was incorporated in 1904. In the last few decades, the growth of the city has not depended on any one industry as it did for the first decades of its existence. Growing to a population of around 35,000 by 1910, the city stayed at that level until the arrival of the I-5 freeway in the 1960s. The post-Vietnam growth of the college and university has also brought in many permanent residents. Exposure to a larger number of visitors has shown off the city's charms and resulted in a steady growth, doubling Bellingham's population through 2008. Expectations are that the city will continue to grow in future years. Hopefully the leaders of the community will preserve the reasons for people coming here to live; the natural beauty, the quiet charm, and of course our wonderful history.

# Bibliography

NEWSPAPERS

Bellingham Herald, The: The Bellingham Herald's Chronological, Anecdotal, and Biographical History of Northwestern Washington supplement to the Bellingham Herald, Bellingham,Wa. 1910 59p Includes a history of Whatcom County by the late Edw. Eldridge, and biographical sketches on John Joseph Donovan, Thomas G. Newman, Charles E. Lind, Edw. Eldridge, J. Pierre Woll, William Cox, Albert E. Mead, Edw. J. Rohrbacher, Fred J. Wood, Syvert H. Johnson, M. D., James Paterson deMattos, C. X. Larrabee, Alvah W. McDonald, Robert J. Glen, Julius H. Bloedel, Homer J. Birney, Robert L. Kline, George W. Mock, Robert F. Hill, Louis D. Brown, Augustus Wilson, Clinton W. Howard, Ed E. Hardin, D. W. Featherkile, James A. Miller, Daniel Campbell, Henry J. Korthauer, Chris Semon, Theodore W. Gillette, John Alonzo Kellogg, K. Sauset, J. M. Ager, et al.

Carhart, Edith Beebe: A History of Bellingham, Washington The Argonaut Press, Bellingham, Wa. 1926 99p (facsimile reproduction by The Shorey Book Store, Seattle, 1968) A compilation of newspaper articles covering the history of Belingham.

Information has also been obtained from the following newspapers:
The Bellingham Bay Mail
The Bellingham Bay Express
The Bellingham Bay Reveille
The Bellingham Herald
The Daily Reveille
The Fairhaven Herald
The Northern Light
The Weekly Blade
The Weekly World

BOOKS

Bancroft, Hubert Howe: Works of H. H. Bancroft volume XXXI History of Washington, Idaho, and Montana 1845-1899 The History Company, San Francisco, California 1890

Biery, Galen, and Koert, Dorothy: Looking Back Vol. 1 Lynden Tribune,Lynden, Wa. 1980 248p A photographic and interview essay.

Biery, Galen, and Koert, Dorothy: Looking Back Vol. 2 Lynden Tribune,Lynden, Wa. 1982 160p

Clark, Donald H.: 18 Men and a Horse Craftsman Press, Seattle, Wa. 1969 215p The story of the Bloedel logging history in the NW.

Coast, The: September 1907 issue of a magazine with articles on Alaska and the Greater Northwest, Vol. 14 No. 3 215p with the whole issue devoted to the Bellingham area.

Edson, Lelah Jackson: The Fourth Corner Craftsman Press, Seattle, Wa. 1968 (originally publ in 1951) 298p A compilation of historical sketches of the Whatcom County area.

Gannaway, Wes; Holsather, Kent: Whatcom Then and Now, A Pictorial History of Whatcom County with an

Emphasis on the Cities on Bellingham Bay during the Centennial Year of Bellingham, 2004 Lone Jack Mountain Press, Bellingham, WA 2004

Jeffcott, Percival R.: Nooksack Tales and Trails Sedro-Woolley Courier-Times, Sedro-Woolley, Wa. 1949 436p A compilation of the history of the northern portion of Whatcom County.

Jukes, Fred; Van Wyck, Philip; Cheever, Bruce B.: The Bellingham Bay and British Columbia Railroad Company The Railway and Locomotive Historical Society, Bulletin No. 84, Baker Library, Harvard Business School, Boston, MA. 1951 77p

Meany, Edmond S.: The Washington Historical Quarterly The Washington University State Historical Society, Seattle, WA April, 1933

Meany, Edmond S.: History of the State of Washington The MacMillan Co., N Y 1946 reprint 412p

Murray, Keith A.: The Story of Banking in Whatcom County privately printed 1954 49p

Polk, R. L. and Co.: Business Directories for Whatcom County for the following years: 1890, 1891, 1899 to 1975

Puget Sound Argus: North-Western Washington, It's Climate, Productions and General Resources Port Townsend, W. T. circa 1880 52p A promotional paper for the counties around the Port Townsend area: Clalam, Island, San Juan, Jefferson and Whatcom (which also included Skagit County at that time.

Roth, Lottie Roeder: History of Whatcom County Washington, Vol. 1 Windmill Publ, Mt. Vernon, Wa. 1992 reprint with index 984p

Roth, Lottie Roeder: History of Whatcom County, Washington, Vo. 2 955p plus index for vol 1 and 2.

Schultz, Louise, editor: Roeder Review 1928 school annual

Scott, James W. and Turbeville III, Daniel E.: Early Industries of Bellingham Bay and Whatcom County Fourth Corner Registry, Bellingham, Wa. 1980 167p

Tetra Tech: Final Report: Bellingham Abandoned Mine Land Survey Tetra Tech, Englewood, Co., 1984, 36p plus appendixes.

Thomas, Robert B. Chuckanut Chronicles Chuckanut Fire Dist. Aux, Bellingham, Wa. 1971 64p Tales of the history around the Chuckanut Bay area.

Turbeville, Daniel E. III: Illustrated Inventory of Historic Bellingham Buildings, 1852-1915 Bell. Muninciple Arts Comm., Bellingham, Wa. 1977 294p A photographic essay of all of the historical buildings of the period still standing in 1977.

Vouri, Michael The Pig War Standoff at Griffin Bay Griffen Bay Bookstore, Friday Harbor, Washington 1999

Whatcom County Souvenir, Bellingham, Washington: circa 1905. evidently a 20 page pamphlet printed in Bellingham for distribution during the Lewis and Clark Centennial Exposition in Portland, Oregon.

## ARCHIVAL RECORDS SOURCES

Center for Pacific Northwest Studies, Goltz-Murray Building, WWU: Various records

Washington State Regional Archives, Goltz-Murray Building, WWU: Various records

Whatcom County Library System Reference Center

University of Washington Special Collections

Washington State Archives, Olympia

## MUSEUMS

Whatcom Museum of History and Art

## GOVERNMENT PUBLICATIONS

Beikman, Helen M., Gower, Howard D., and Dana, Toni A.: Coal Reserves of Washington DNR Bulletin 47, Olympia, Wa. 1961 with addendum by Schasse, Henry W., Walsh, Timothy J., and Phillips, Wm. M. 1984 115p Describes coal production and reserves to date in Washignton State.

Knoblach, David A.: Washington's Stone Industry-A History Washington Geology, vol.21, no.4, Olympia, Wa. Dec. 1993 pp3-17

Turbeville, Daniel E. III: The Electric Railway Era in Northwest Washington, 1890-1930 Occasional Paper No. 12, Center for Pacific NW Studies, WWU, Bellingham, Wa. 1977 198p.

United States Environmental Protection Agency Sehome Mine Preliminary Assessment Trip Report Bellingham, Washington TDD: 03-01-0002 Seattle. Wa. 2004

Vonheeder, Ellis R.: Coal Reserves of Whatcom County, Washington Washington State Dept. of Natural Resources, Div. of Land Management, Olympia, Wa., 1975, 85p.

# Index

Aftermath Club (Broadway Hall) 20, 22, 160, 161
Akers, Carl and Nicki 14, 15
Akers Taxidermy 14
Akin, J. N. and L. Agnes
Alaska Block 123, 124, 186
Alexander, James 12
Antler Hotel 128
Assumption Catholic Church 133, 136, 137
Assumption School 136
Austin, H. 10
Bacon, George 201
Bahia de Gascon 40
Baker Hotel (Grand Central Hotel) 71, 120, 121, 162-164, 205
Bancroft, Hubert H. 42
Barkhousen, H. C. 9
Barnum and Bailey Circus 184
Barrett, Sam 55
Bartlett, Erastus 72, 106, 194, 202
Base Camp sporting goods store 14
Bausman, William 12, 58
Bean, L. H. 22
Beck, Jacob 127
Bellingham Amusement Company 91
Bellingham Bay throughout the book, especially page 40
Bellingham Bay Brewery (3B Brewery) 183
Bellingham Bay Coal Company 9, 43, 45, 62, 116
Bellingham Bay and Eastern RR 76, 108
Bellingham Bay & British Columbia Railroad Company (BB&BC) 20, 24, 62, 64, 70, 76, 77, 79, 108, 116, 117, 118, 203, 204
Bellingham Bay Express newspaper 64
Bellingham Bay Grocery 70, 76
Bellingham Bay Improvement Company (BBIC) 62, 80, 116, 121, 196, 203, 207
Bellingham Bay Improvement Company Mill 80, 107, 108, 130, 176, 178, 208
Bellingham Bay Mail newspaper 13
Bellingham Bay National Bank (Pike Block) 71, 121, 122, 130
Bellingham High School 143, 146, 183
Bellingham Hotel (Bellingham Tower) 168
Bellingham Labor Council 127
Bellingham National Guard 20, 24
Bellingham Sash and Door Company 110
Bellingham School District Administrative Office 143
Bellingham State Band 24
Benham, Calhoun 60
Bennett, John 45, 115
Bennett, Nelson 72, 75, 77, 88, 106, 202
Betschart and Steiner Building 127
Black, A. L. 17, 22
Bloedel, Julius H. 107, 108, 109, 166

Bloedel Donovan Mill 108, 109, 137
Bloedel Donovan Cargo Mill 108
Bloedel Park 188
Bloomquist, N. F. 10
Blue Canyon Coal Dock 51
Blue Canyon Coal Mine 76
Bolster Home 80
Boulevard Park 106
Bradshaw, C. M. 10
Brewery Fair Grounds 183
Broadway Park 165, 207
Brooks, Bill 14
Brown, Henry C. 42, 43, 60, 61, 106
Brown, Samuel 42, 43, 45, 60, 61
Builder's Alliance 110
Buswell, Howard 12, 15
Canadian Pacific RR (CPR) 76, 77, 177
Carnegie Library iii
Center for Pacific Northwest Studies 15
Central High School 142
Chandler, C. H. 91, 92, 93, 94
Chicago Milwaukie St Paul and Pacific (Milwaukie Line) RR 76, 77
Chowitzan, one of the Lummi Chiefs (name spelled various ways) 42
Chuckanut Brewery 65
Chuckanut Sandstone Quarry 148
Cissna, Charles 170
Citizens Dock 177, 179
Clark Plumbing and Heating 127
Clayton, Joel 46
Clover Block 86
Coleman, Edmund T. 117
Colony Dock 66, 110, 111
Colony Mill 43, 63, 66, 67, 106, 109, 110
Columbia Valley Lumber Company 109
Community Food Co-op
Compton, Enoch 44, 45
Cornwall, Pierre B. 51, 54, 61, 62, 76, 106, 116. 203, 204
Cory, Clyde and Margaret 149
Cougar Club (upstairs in the Roehl Block) 17, 24
Cozy Apartments 127
Dahlquist Building 126, 128, 129
Dahlquist Grocery Company 126, 128
Day, E. P. Y. 22
Daylight Block 124
deLacy, W. W. 50
DeMattos, James Patterson 10, 17, 19, 22, 166
Deming, E. B. 22, 162, 164
Dibble, Carmin 200
Dickenson, H. L. 17, 22, 23

Dobbs, Beverly 49, 120
Dobbs and Fleming Photographers 120
Donovan, Charles 8
Donovan-Flynn Automobile Company 162
Donovan, John J. 24, 79, 107, 108, 109, 202
Doty, Seth 46
Douglas Block 168
Douglas, Governor James 5, 6, 12, 49, 50
Dufner, Nick 10
Durkee, Mrs. I. M. 10
East Broadway Park
Ebert, Max and Emma 149
Ebey, Isaac 40
Edson, Lelah Jackson 15, 49, 57
Eliza, Francisco 38
E. K. Wood Mill 19, 22, 112, 194
Eldridge, Edward 13, 38, 42, 44, 45, 46, 48, 50, 72, 106, 148, 192, 194, 202
Eldridge, Hugh 55
Eldridge, Isabella 42, 48
Eldridge, Teresa 42, 44, 46
Elk Hotel 127
Elk's Club 17, 24
Elmheim Mansion 148-153
"Elsinore" 102
Esquimalt, B. C. 43
E Street Wharf 58
Exchange Block (YMCA) 25, 123, 124
Fairhaven and New Whatcom Railway Company 83
Fairhaven and Northern RR 76, 77
Fairhaven and Southern RR 72, 76, 77, 108, 175
Fairhaven Hotel 73, 75
Fairhaven Improvement Company 88, 193, 202
Fairhaven Land Company 72, 202
Fairyland Skating Rink 134
Father Blanchet 40
Father Boulet 48
Fauntleroy, W. H. 43, 44, 45
Federal Building iii, 166-168
Fenton, Richard 206
Ferndale 38
Finkbonner, C. C. 13
First Christian Church 159
First National Bank of Fairhaven 108
First National Bank of Whatcom 70, 148
First Presbyterian Church 71
Fisher, Edward 69
Fitzhugh, Edmund C. 9, 45, 47, 48, 49, 50, 61, 189
Fort Bellingham 37, 45, 47, 49, 58
Fort Langley 39

Fort Victoria, Victoria B. C. 37, 38, 39, 42, 43, 46, 50, 57, 62
Friday Harbor 38, 57
Gage, George 149
Gamwell, Roland 17, 72, 80
"General Harney" 50
Geneva Mill 109
Georgia Pacific 111
Glazer, Burton 150
Globe Mill 106, 176
Great Northern RR (GN) 72, 76, 77, 112, 176, 202
Great White Fleet 16 – 36, 91, 92
Guthrie, Jimmy 52
Gwinn, William 91, 92
Hadley, F. E. 22
Haggard, Harvey iii
Handschy, Frank 49
Harris, Dan 10, 13, 45, 72, 75, 106, 175, 193, 202
Harte, W. M. 10
Hastings Mill 108
Heath, John 41
Hedge, J. D. 42, 43, 44
Hegg, E. A. 69, 107, 117
Hegg, Peter 107
Henika, Ethel 95
Herald Building 124, 132
Hewitt, Henry 42, 43, 45, 60, 61
"H C Page" 37, 45, 47, 48
Higgenson, Ella 86
Holtzheimer, Edward 10
Howard, William A 42
Hudson Bay Company (HBC) 39, 40, 49
Hyatt, G. C. 22
Hyatt, John G. 8 – 15
Interstate 5 171-173
Irving Hotel 127
Iverson, O. B. 199
Jeffcott, P. R. 15
Jehova's Witness church 14
Jenkins, D. C. 199
Jenkins, Elizabeth 199
Jenkins, Elvira (Mrs. Will Jenkins) 10, 199
Jenkins, John 55
Jenkins, Will D. 10
Jerns Mill 109
Jones and Carlyon Real Estate 64, 120, 131, 162, 205
Jones, Reginald 90
Jones, Thomas 44
Junior Order of American Mechanics 14
Keystone Hotel (old Sehome Hotel) 46, 55, 70, 118, 119, 131
Kalloch, H. K. 10

Kavanaugh, James also Cavenaugh 9, 10, 12
Kellogg, George A. 17, 55, 201
Kindall, J. W. 22
"Kulshan" 177
Kulshan Club (in Fairhaven) 17, 24
Lake Whatcom Logging Company 108
Lake Whatcom Motor Club 170
Larrabee, C. X. 72
Larson Mill 96, 108
Larson, Peter 108
Laube Block 125
Laurel Park Playground 70
Leach, David 46
Leckie, Stuart 10
Lee, Alfred 84, 85
Lighthouse, J. C. Block 70
Loggie, George 109, 186
Loggie, Helen 186
Loggie, J. W. 22
Loggie Mill 109, 111
Loop's Ranch 114
Lummi Natives 39, 46, 48
Lysle, John 44, 45
Lysle, Mary 46
Ma-Mo-Sea Coal Mine, voting precinct 45, 46
Manifest Destiny 39
Maritime Park 81
Mason Block 79
Mayhew, Mrs. M. H. 10
McAlpine, Edward 10
McCaddon and Phillips Ice Cream Shop 31
McClean, Alexander 61
McCue Mill 108
McCush, Dan 22
McLeod Block 123, 124
McMackin, P. A. 10
McPherson, Mrs. R. Merriam 10
Merrin, George and Selma 149, 150
Mills, D. O. 61
Milwaukie RR Roundhouse 51, 52
Model Truck and Storage Company 127
Monahan Building 79
Montague and McHugh Department Store 168
Moody, William 9, 12
Morgan Block 79
Morning Mist 47
Morrison, James 40, 42, 43, 44, 45
Morrison Mill 69, 106, 111, 178
Morse Hardware 88, 118

Morse, Robert Home 80, 85
Mount Baker 38
Mount Baker Apartments (Cissna Apartments) 78, 168
Mount Baker Marathon iii
Mullin Hotel 128, 129
National Guard (Company F, First Infantry Regiment) 132, 134
National Guard Armory 133, 134, 135
New China Café 128
Newsome, D. F. 46
New Westminster and Southern RR 76, 77
New Whatcom City Hall (Bellingham City Hall) 66, 78, 84
Noble, J. N. 94, 95
Nooksack Natives 39
Nootka Sound 38
North Coast Transportation Company (Greyhound) 130
Northern Hotel (first Fairhaven Hotel) 75
Northern Light newspaper 58
Northern Pacific RR (NP) 76, 77, 108, 112
North Side High School 142, 144, 145, 147
Norwegian Lutheran Church iii
Ocean Dock 175
O'Conner, Maurice 44, 45
Offat, M. H. 9
Ogden, Peter Skene 39
Orchard Terrace 69, 116, 118, 119, 121
Pacific American Fisheries (PAF) 75, 130, 164
Pacific Atomized Fuel Company 95
Page, Henry C. 44, 45
Pantage's Theater 124
Pattle's Point 42
Pattle, William 40, 42, 43, 44, 45, 46
Patton, H. W. 22
Peabody Hill 46, 50
Peabody, John 62
Peabody, Russell V. throughout the book
Pentland, E. C. 10
Pentland, Mrs. E. C. 10
Pettibone, C. J. 62, 106, 195, 197
Phelps, L. G. Building 11, 62, 63
Pickett Bridge 67, 68, 197
Pickett, George 12, 37, 38, 45, 46, 47, 48, 49, 50, 58, 115
Pickett, James Tilton 47
Pig War 38
Pitchford, William 55
Pitchford, Mrs. William 55
Plummer, Alfred 41, 42
Poe, Alonzo M. 8, 11, 38, 40, 44, 50, 190, 191
Poe's Point 40, 42
Point Roberts 39
Post Point 40

Powell, Mrs. J. G. 10
Powers, James 13, 55
Prather, E. C. 62, 196
Puget Sound Coal Mine Association 42
Puget Sound Mill (Earles and Cleary Mill) 112, 113
Puget Sound Power Traction and Light (Puget Sound Power and Light, Puget Sound Power, Puget Sound Energy) 83, 122, 130
Puget Sound Pulp and Timber Company 111
Purdy, E. W. 24, 26
Quackenbush Block 64, 79
Radley, Lt. 23, 24
Red Front Block 29, 87
Red Mill (Eldridge Bartlett Mill) 106, 112, 194
Richards, Charles E. 8 - 15
Richards, Thomas G. 11- 15, 46, 50
Riddle, Jasper M. 14
Ringling Brothers Circus 180-186
Roberts, C. E. 44, 45, 47
Roberts, Maria 46
Roeder, Elizabeth 46, 60, 148
Roeder Grade School 142
Roeder, Henry throughout the book
Roeder, Henry Jr. 55
Roeder Junior High School 143
Rogue Hero Tavern 128
Roth Block 80
Roth, Charles Independence 80, 148, 149, 166
Roth, Lottie Roeder 15, 48, 54, 55, 60, 148, 149
Saint Joseph Hospital 137-141
Saint Lukes Hospital 137
Samish Lake Logging Company 108
Seattle and Northern RR 76
Seattle Lakeshore and Eastern RR 72, 76, 77
Sehome, Sub-Chief 45, 48, 117
Sehome Coal Mine 38, 45, 51, 53, 56, 117, 118
Sehome Coal Mine Company 45, 203
Sehome Dock 117, 118, 163, 174, 178
Sehome Hotel (1888) 119
Sehome School 70, 118
Schmidt, Leopold 127
Siemens Mill 88
Sigfred, J. W. 10
Silver Beach 30, 31, 90- 104, 120, 188, 205
Silver Beach Hotel 90- 104, 120, 205
Simpson, Goldie E. 149
Simpson, Holly and Goldie 149
S'Klallam (Clallam Tribe) 117
Slade Real Estate Company Building 125, 131
Slater, John 55
S-mas (Sumas) Natives 39

Smith Dairy 86
South Hill Apartments 141
Stangroom, Marc LaRiviere 69, 106, 107
Stead, Elgia M. 98
Steadman, James B.; Post #24 14
Stenger, John 62, 65, 106
Sterns, Rufus 10
Stone and Webster 83, 122, 130
Stuabbs, S. D. 10
Sunset Block 25, 28, 71, 79, 121, 123, 126
Swan's Moving Company 162
Swanton's (dance hall on the upper floor of the Fair Market) 17
Swedish Baptist Church
Tawes, Mary 48
Tawes, McKinney 48
Taylor, James 45, 48, 50
Taylor, James Knox 166
Technocracy Inc. 127
Tegenfeldt and Farquharson Plumbing and Heating 127
Tennant, John A. 9
Terminal Building 73, 79
Territorial Courthouse Task Force 14
Thayer, Clarence 112
Thomas, John 40, 42, 43, 44, 45
Thornton, Dr. A. W. 13
Tom's Beaver Inn 127, 128
Tuck, D. E. 10
Tuck, Elizabeth 55
Turner, James O. 9
T. G. Richards Building, Brick Courthouse 5 – 15, 57, 58
USS Constitution 154-158
Utter, William 37, 42, 44, 45, 48, 61
Vail, Charles C. 43, 44, 45, 48, 189
Vancouver, George 39
Vernon, Mrs. F. A. 10
Waldron Block 79, 85
Warbuss, E. D. 49, 50
Wardner, James 72, 79, 108
Washington Colony 62
Washington School 71
Washington Treaty 36
Waterfront Tavern 65
Watson, Flip-Flap-Flop 10
Weise, J. H. 166
Weisenburger, Col. John J. 134
Western Washington University (State Normal School, Bellingham Normal School, W W College) (WWU) 85, 134
Westford, Jack 160
Whatcom Bank 62
Whatcom Brewery 127

Whatcom County Courthouse 57, 70
Whatcom County Railway and Light 83, 93
Whatcom Falls Mill, Roeder Mill, Whatcom Milling Company, Whatcom Falls Mill Company (several names for the same mill) 9, 43, 51, 57, 58, 59, 60, 62
Whatcom High School 143, 146
Whatcom Historical Society 150
Whatcom House Hotel 55, 58
Whatcom Junior High School 143, 146
Whatcom Middle School 143, 146, 147
Whatcom Museum of History and Art 15, 84
Whatcom Post Office 59
Whatcom Reveille newspaper 62, 66, 78, 80
White City 17, 24, 25, 30, 31, 90- 105
Wilkes, Charles 39
William Tell Hotel 127
William Tell Saloon 127
Winsor Hotel 125
Wood, Edwin Kleber 106, 112
Wood, Fred 112
Wyman, S. D. 106
York Band 90-104, 166

Born and raised in Bellingham, Washington, Kent Holsather has had a lifelong obsession for the history of Bellingham and Whatcom County. Introduced to local history by his third grade teacher, he has found that his interest of the past has only grown more intense as the years have gone by.

Recently retired, he spends much of his time volunteering at the Whatcom Museum of History and Art where he loves spending time digging up and identifying old photos from the archives. He has authored two historical fiction novels and has co-authored two historical books with his close friend, Wes Gannaway.

His hobbies include softball, drumming, trivia games and watching college football. He also writes occasional personal essays for a writer's website "Thecolumnists.com"

He and his wife have been married for 31 years. They were blessed recently with the arrival of their first grandchild.


Wes Gannaway grew up in Darrington, Washington (a very historical saw mill town), and Ballard, a suburb of Seattle, although he likes to think of Ballard as a separate city. Wes became fascinated with history when he found out that his grandfather was a cowboy. Wes moved with his family to Ferndale in 1971 to work at the ARCO refinery. While studying the geology of the area, Wes found photos of the buildings constructed with sandstone from the Roeder Quarry and he went from there into the general history of Whatcom County. His desire to pass on the memories of the old days has led him to be on the board of the Whatcom Historical Society and work toward the restoration of the old Richards brick building.

His hobbies include traveling to old mining towns to explore the mines and collect ore samples. He also visits any museums along the way.

Wes has given several talks on various local history topics and has co-authored "Whatcom Then and Now" and "Bellingham Then and Now" with Kent Holsather.

Wes is semi-retired, and lives in Ferndale with his wife of 41 years, and his grandson.